AMERICAN ENVIRONMENTAL STUDIES

Pittsburgh
In The Year 1826

SAMUEL JONES

———————————————

ARNO &
THE NEW YORK TIMES

Collection Created and Selected
by CHARLES GREGG of Gregg Press

Reprint Edition 1970 by Arno Press Inc.

Reprinted from a microfilm copy
furnished by The Columbia University Library

LC# 70-125749
ISBN 0-405-02673-0

American Environmental Studies
ISBN for complete set: 0-405-02650-1

Manufactured in the United States of America

PITTSBURGH

IN THE YEAR

EIGHTEEN HUNDRED AND TWENTY-SIX

J.H.H. inv. et del.

Savory Sc. Pitt.

TRINITY CHURCH, PITTSBURGH.
Founded A.D. 1824.

PITTSBURGH

IN THE YEAR

EIGHTEEN HUNDRED AND TWENTY-SIX,

CONTAINING

SKETCHES

TOPOGRAPHICAL, HISTORICAL AND STATISTICAL;

TOGETHER WITH

A DIRECTORY OF THE CITY,

AND

A VIEW OF ITS VARIOUS MANUFACTURES, POPULATION, IMPROVEMENTS, &c.

Embellished with an Engraving of the Episcopal Church.

BY S. JONES.

Pittsburgh:

PRINTED BY JOHNSTON & STOCKTON.

....

1826.

PREFACE.

IT is now SEVEN years since a work of this description was published in Pittsburgh, and although the patronage extended towards it at that time, was but a miserable remuneration for the trouble and labour attendant on its execution, it has been thought that the increase of the City, as well in its business as its population, would certainly warrant the present publication—but, alas!

"Who ever reads an American book."

The subscription lists present but a bare security for the incidental expenses. I will not, however, trouble my readers with a long prologue of complaints. As the work was undertaken for amusement, to fill up some leisure hours, with a desire, at the same time, of making it a vehicle of much useful information, it shall go to press. The book may have many defects, such things being almost unavoidable in works got up within circumscribed periods. However, all diligence has been paid, and, as far as my humble, and very limited capabilities extend, they have been employed in laying before the public eye, such a view of Pittsburgh, in relation to its various points of interest, as has been thought useful and entertaining.

It has been said, that some books have a redeeming quality in the beauty of their pictures—therefore taking due cognizance of that fact, I present ONE, from the able pencil of the Rev. J. H. HOPKINS, trusting, that should the critical acumen of any of my gentle readers be started, they will duly consider my FRONTISPIECE.

To those gentlemen who kindly contributed information and assistance in the various departments, I tender my acknowledgments.— To the FEW who refused, and it is gratifying that the number is but few, I am under no obligations; and I take the liberty of mentioning to them, that the withholding of such information in relation to their business as might interest the public, and show the spirit and enterprize of the place, is strongly indicative of those miserable fears of exciting competition, which are the offspring of a policy as narrow-hearted as discreditable.

S. J.

PITTSBURGH.

TOPOGRAPHICAL.

THE Editor would flatter himself as possessing considerable originality, were he able to advance any thing new as it regards a description of Pittsburgh. Its peculiar and happy situation, and its prominence as a manufacturing town, have already rendered it the subject of many well written publications, which have embraced almost every point of interest about its location. To those too, who reside on the spot, and in a work so purely local as the present, a lengthy and protracted description of that which is every day before the eye, may be deemed as scarcely necessary; but as these pages may possibly stray into other countries, and into the hands of those persons who have only *heard* of Pittsburgh, and who are ignorant of her localities and peculiar natural advantages, some remarks on the topography of the city and the surrounding country, may not be inapposite; and although an exact repetition of what has been before written, is not very desirable, still much information has been derived from those papers, and which must necessarily form some part of this sketch.

In addition to the geographical notice of Pittsburgh, some remarks will be made on the rivers and face of the country in their immediate neighbourhood. The great æra of internal improvement now commenced, has rendered almost every thing connected with it (the rivers particularly) worthy of attention and observation.

PITTSBURGH is one of the manor tracts, which the Legislature of Pennsylvania, during the Session of 1779, confirmed to the descendants of William Penn. The town was laid out by Col. George Woods, in 1784. It

1*

embraces the immediate point of land formed by the confluence of the Allegheny and Monongahela rivers, which
streams constitute the Ohio. In 40° 31' 44" N. Latitude, and 80° 8' West Longitude.

"The City has four unequal sides, but is very nearly a
regular right angle triangle; the side bordering on the
Allegheny being the longest, and the line from one river
to the other, on the East side, the shortest of the three.
The longest side is nearly a mile, and the shortest, nearly
three quarters of a mile. The principal streets join the
Monongahela at right angles, and these are intersected
nearly at right angles by others running parallel to the
Monongahela. On the North, or rather North-western
side of these, are two ranges of squares parallel with the
Allegheny, which, of course, join the other streets and
squares at irregular angles."

Pittsburgh is built upon a plain, rising above the level
of the rivers, at low-water mark, about thirty or forty feet;
the lowest part being on the side next the Allegheny.
This low part was once a very extensive flat, several hundred yards in breadth, but owing to the rapid current of
the river, during the numerous freshets, and the soft and
earthy nature of its banks, a great part of it has been
washed away. Along the whole extent of the banks of
either river, within the bounds of the city, there is scarcely a single rock or stone, if we except the gravel on the
immediate beach of the Allegheny; sand and clay being
the constituent parts of all the ground upon which the city is built, for a considerable depth. The earth is supposed to be alluvion.

So well surrounded is Pittsburgh with hills, that it
may be justly supposed to resemble the area a vast am-
phitheatre. On the South side of the Monongahela, and
immediately opposite the city, arises Coal Hill, presenting a steep, rugged and rocky front, which in the winter
season, exhibits a very bleak and dreary aspect; but in
summer and autumn, it is extremely beautiful, owing to
the thick and verdant foliage of the thousand trees and
shrubs that seem to grow on the very rocks. The highest
altitude of this Hill (nearly opposite to Ferry street) is
465 feet. It extends, unbroken, for several miles up and
down the river. In that part of the hill above the Pittsburgh Glass-works, and near its summit, there has been
fire burning for many years, and the smoke may be seen

daily curling from out the fissures of the rocks. The fire is in the midst of the great strata of coal that here stretches along the hill. How this fire originated is pretty much of a desideratum, and many conjectures have been expressed; but the greatest probability is, that as it is common for the diggers to have large fires at the mouth of the pits, there must have been one here, which on the pit's being abandoned for a time, was left burning, and by degrees, through the great quantity of slack or fine coal usually thrown about, worked its way into the pit itself. Frequent attempts have been made to suppress the burning, by stopping up the mouth of the mine and neighbouring crevices, to prevent the accession of air, but in vain—it still rages, and is daily extending, and may some day produce serious consequences.

On the back or Eastern part of the city, are Grant's and Boyd's Hills.—The first is within the precincts, and is partly in a state of lawn; its height is only about 70 feet. The second, is on the boundary line; commencing its rise not far from the Monongahela, along which it soon extends for about two miles; one mile of which is composed of rocky and perpendicular precipices of an hundred feet in height—From the summits of these, it slopes gradually towards Grant's Hill, forming a small, but beautiful belt of land, which is devoted to small farms and summer residences. On the North-east part of the city, and adjoining Grant's Hill, where it rises with a gradual ascent, is Quarry Hill, whence the principal part of all the stone used in Pittsburgh has been taken—from its point, which is just within the city, it extends along and binds the second flat of the Allegheny, for about two miles, when it is broken by the ravine of the two-mile run. The aspect of this Hill on the West side, is very barren and poor, presenting scarcely any thing else than stone-quarries. The top and opposite side is composed of a tolerable good soil, but is poorly cultivated. Here are a great number of coal-pits. The highest elevation of Quarry Hill is about 440 feet. On the Western side of the Allegheny, and opposite the lower part of the city, is an abrupt promontory, called Hogback Hill, from its peculiar formation. It is about half a mile in length, and is of little value. In the rear of this hill, and running North and South, is the great chain of hills that bind the flat lands on the Allegheny and Ohio.

In all these elevations, coal is found in immense quantities—except in Grant's, Boyd's, and Hogback hills; their altitude not being sufficient to bring them within the range of the great strata of that mineral which pervades this region of country.

The scenery around Pittsburgh is very beautiful, and when viewed from some points, presents the most interesting associations of nature and art. The view from Castleman's Hill, is not surpassed in any country—earth, air, rock, wood, water, town and sky, break upon the vision in forms the most picturesque and delightful. Coal Hill, immediately above the burning pits, is another point of interesting observation, where the eye, at a single glance, takes in an hundred beauties, which might vie with the purest and brightest of the other hemisphere.

Pittsburgh has several suburban villages, that contribute to, and are supplied from the great *centre*, with which their strength and prosperity are intimately connected.

On, or nearly adjoining the North-eastern boundary of the city, and on the flat between Quarry Hill and the Allegheny river, the NORTHERN LIBERTIES are situated, and are intended as a continuation of Pittsburgh. They were laid out in 1816, by Geo. A. Bayard, and James Adams. The lots were originally let on perpetual leases, and such was the eagerness of persons to obtain property at that time, that from one and a half to two dollars per foot were readily given. However, the consequences of the peace—the ruinous policy of the banking system, at that time in vogue, and the numerous train of evils which ever follow a depression of enterprize, rendered many of the leasees unable to pay their rents, notwithstanding many of them had put up comfortable habitations. The proprietors were, therefore, obliged to take back many of their lots. Yet the village has lost none of its population as to numbers—it is now improving rapidly, and contains the Phœnix Cotton Factory, Juniata Iron Works, &c.

Adjoining the South-eastern boundary of the city, on the Monongahela, stands KENSINGTON, or as it is commonly called, *Pipe-town;* deriving this name through one of its early settlers, an eccentric little gentleman, still well known among all classes, for his odd humour, and the universality of his mechanical genius, Mr. *William Price,* who established a Pipe manufactory there. Kensington is composed of lots laid out by several individuals, which run from the road, or extension of Second street, to the river —and to every one it presents matter of surprise, how so ungainly a situation should be thought of, not only for private dwellings, but for extensive manufactories, as there is not, if we except the lower corner, on Suke's Run, naturally, thirty feet square of level ground, in the whole place—Yet, there are here, two steam rolling-mills, a wire manufactory, an air foundry, a steam grist-mill, a steam engine for turning and grinding brass and iron, and a brewery.

A short distance above Kensington, on the South and opposite side of the river, stand BIRMINGHAM, and SIDNEYVILLE, which may be considered the southern suburbs of Pittsburgh. These villages were laid out by Dr. Nathaniel Bedford and Mr. Isaac Gregg. The name of Sidneyville, however, has been lost in that of Birmingham, as the latter is now applied to both. For several years after the location of these villages, which was in 1811, they increased quite rapidly, but latterly, their increase has been very gradual. It is here that the well known Birmingham Glass is manufactured. There are also here, a steam grist-mill, and an extensive lock manufactory. By an Act of the late Legislature, Birmingham was incorporated into a borough.

On the Western side of the Allegheny, on the second bottom, a few hundred yards from the shore, is the TOWN OF ALLEGHENY. This place was laid out by order of the Supreme Executive Council of Pennsylvania, in 1789. It is an exact square, and consists only of an hundred in-lots. 60 by 240 feet. The out-lots, however, are very numerous, containing from eight to ten acres each—they extend a considerable distance up the Allegheny, and down the Ohio about two miles and a half. embracing several thousand acres, which were denominated the *Reserved Tract.* The town is connected with Pittsburgh, by the Allegheny bridge, and is a great thoroughfare, as here, all the principal highways, leading to and from the North and West, concentrate. It is here also, that the Western Penitentiary of Pennsylvania, is erected, which for workmanship and excellence of design, is not surpassed by any building of the kind in the United States. The form is that of an octagon, enclosing an area of about two acres and three fourths. The main. or front building, is 122 feet in length, and 46 feet high, and flanked by two circular towers, all surmounted with battlements. The surrounding wall is 25 feet in height, and has two other towers, placed equi-distant from the main building. The whole is built of hewn stone, and exhibits very much the appearance of an ancient castle. The massy grating of the windows and the indented mason work, give it rather a gloomy and sombre aspect—but, altogether, it is a very majestic and formidable pile. As solitary confinement, without any kind of labour, is contemplated in this prison, the greater part of the ground enclosed, has been built up with cells. Of these, there are 192. They are built of brick and stone ; are one story high, and form a very beautiful circle. The cells are each 6 feet by 8, with a large iron ring in the centre, to which the convict will be chained; and as a further security, each apartment is provided with double doors—one on the inside, of wood, with a small opening, for the admission of light, air, and provision; the other, on the outside, of heavy bar iron, with ingenious and powerful fastenings.—Here will the victim of crime have to expiate his offences in a manner that must convey more terror to the minds of wicked men than all the systems of punishment devised in our country. Immured, and shut out almost from the light of heaven; cut off from all intercourse with his fellow creatures, not even the voice of his keeper, will ever break upon his solitude, nor will he see him, except, when through the little wicket of his prison door, he tenders the means of sustenance—without books, without tools, without any thing to lull and soothe that conscience, which, like an eternal and undying worm, must prey upon his heart; in short, without even a nail to etch upon the wall, another day to those which he has spent there, will the criminal have to drag out the term of his miserable incarceration. Every thing relative to the Penitentiary, has been done in that elegant and substantial manner which reflects great credit on *Mr. Evans*, the architect, and Messrs. *Hannen* and *Fairman* the builders. Convicts will, probably, be received this year. The establishment will have cost, when completed, about 180 000 dollars.

Two miles above Pittsburgh, on the Eastern shore of the Allegheny, is the village of LAWRENCEVILLE ; laid out in the year 1815, by William B. Foster.—Its commencement and progress were identified with the erection of the U.

S. Arsenal, which is located on a stripe of land, running from the river, and occupying the centre of the village. The population, amounting to nearly 200, are principally engaged about the public works. The Arsenal and buildings connected with it, form an elegant group, and were built under the superintendance of Major A. R. Woolley. The mounting of ordnance, and the making and repairing of various arms and military accoutrements, are the entire employments of the artizans engaged or enlisted. There are, at present, a company of artillerists stationed here, and the whole is under the command of Major Churchill.

But to return to the city—Its appearance is far from being prepossessing; the everlasting cloud of smoke that hovers over it, and the black and sooty countenance of every thing, animate and inanimate, render it not unlike an immense smith-shop. The houses are without any kind of regularity; on one square may be seen a handsome block of brick buildings, occupied by merchants and private families, while, on the next, is a row of one and two story frames, some with their sides, and others with their gable ends on the street, exhibiting a motley assemblage of cordwainers, small dealers, and no small number of those *interesting places of refreshment*, termed *grocery and liquor stores*. Nearly the whole town is built in this way. Why it is so, cannot be explained, unless it be said that it was intended to realize a line of the old song—

"Variety is charming."

Of late years, great improvements have been made by paving those streets, that were formerly deep and dirty. Paved side-walks are very general throughout, and as the city progresses, attention to various objects of utility, connected with cleanliness, will, doubtless, be paid. The completion of the contemplated Water Works, will be of immense advantage, not only in cases of fire, or private convenience, but in cleansing the streets and pavements, and in the summer, rendering the city cool and less dusty.

Pittsburgh, being situated in the centre of a large and extensive country, whose population are, in a great measure, dependant on her for a market for their produce, and who regard her as the great store-house, whence to draw their supplies; with an hundred roads leading towards her, through her great highways, is always filled with a numerous concourse of strangers, of all classes, countries.

and denominations.   The spring and fall, however, are
the most busy periods ; yet, at all times, the city exhibits
great bustle and activity ; the rattling of drays, carts and
wagons ; the puffing of steam ; the noise of machinery,
and the continued tread of the passing multitude, indicate
the industry and extensive business of the place.

In matters of taste, in relation to their public and private buildings, the Pittsburghers have but little to boast.
The Episcopal church, of which a drawing is presented, is
by far the handsomest edifice in the city.   The others are
very ordinary and common place, being built more for
cheapness than ornament.   As to literary institutions, if
we except the Medical Society, and Apprentices' Library
Association, there are none.

Of the *Allegheny* and *Monongahela* rivers, we shall now
speak at scme length ; a new importance, as was before
observed, having been given to these streams, by the en-
actment of the late canal bills in the Legislatures of Pennsylvania and Maryland.

The Allegheny, at Pittsburgh, is about 1100 feet in
width, over which there is a bridge thrown from St. Clair
street, of 6 arches, each 187 feet span, elevated about 32
feet above the level of low water.   This river, with its
beautiful pebbly channel, and chrystal waters, as is observed in a well written article, from the pen of an intel-
ligent member of the society for the promotion of internal
improvement, rises in Potter county, Pennsylvania, and
Cataragus, in New York, fifty miles from the Pennsylvania line.   It receives in its course, the Conewango creek,
along which boats constantly navigate from Chataque
Lake, in New-York, the head of which is but eight miles
from Lake Erie ; the Tionesta creek, navigable at some
seasons with rafts, for upwards of fifty miles above its
junction with the river, and rises in Warren, M'Kean,
Jefferson, and Venango counties ; French creek, a stream
which is navigable, in the spring and autumn, to Waterford, a distance of sixty miles from its junction with the
Allegheny at Franklin, and which passes through the fertile counties of Erie, Crawford and Venango ; Scrubgrass
creek, which rises in Venango and Butler counties ; To-
by's creek, or Clarion river, which takes its rise in M'Kean
county, and is almost united with some of the sources of
the Susquehanna, and passes through Jefferson, Venango,

and Armstrong; Sandy lick and Mahoning creek, the fountains of which are in M'Kean, Clearfield, and Indiana counties, and which fertilize in their way Jefferson and Armstrong; Kiskeminitas, a navigable stream, the heads of which interlock with the west branch of the Susquehanna, the Juniata, and the Youghiogany; and whose banks abound with strong springs of Salt water, upon which extensive manufactories of that article are established.

The Allegheny is navigable, when the waters of the west are increased by the melting of the snows of the winter, from Hamilton, in N. York, to Pittsburgh, a distance of about 270 miles. By a short portage between Chataque Lake and Portland, on Erie, along the bed of the Conewango, to the Allegheny, at or near Warren, a communication may be formed with the lake. Were it not for this portage, nineteen of the United States would be surrounded with water. The dividing ridge at this point is 860 feet above Lake Erie, and 300 above the Chataque. The low water mark of the Ohio, at Pittsburgh, is 152 feet above Lake Erie, 727 above the Hudson at Albany, and 756 above the Atlantic Ocean, at Cape May.

Descending the Allegheny from the Pennsylvania line to Pittsburgh, are found the towns of Warren, the beauty of which, from its situation, is conceded by all; Franklin, at the mouth of French creek, destined to become the Rochester of Pennsylvania; Lawrenceburgh, seated like an eagle's nest among the hills, opposite the mouth of Clarion river; and Kittanning, a neat and prosperous town on the bank of the river, in the midst of a fine and improving country.

Ascending French creek, 35 miles by water, we find the town of Meadville. It is situated on the left bank of the stream, and is one of the most flourishing villages in Pennsylvania. A large and elegant building has been erected for a college, which, with a fair portion of legislative patronage, will, at no distant day, be a most valuable seminary of learning. A court-house, upon a plan liberally presented by Mr. Strickland, is nearly completed, and which will become a model for public buildings in the west.

French creek is navigable at some seasons to Waterford, 85 miles (by water) from the river, and the distance from Waterford to Erie is but 15 miles. It is well known that at Erie, the joint efforts of the state and general govern-

2

ments, are directed to the improvement of the harbour, and there is every expectation that it will be made the best upon the lake.

Taken in a state of nature, the Allegheny and its branches are the recipients of the northern part of the great western basin of Pennsylvania, and but little impeded by falls, though rapid as to current, from the declivity of their plane of motion.

Upon the banks of this river, and those of its tributary streams, bituminous coal, rich iron ore, and limestone abound. Water power, to any extent, is found every where; and already capital and enterprize are extensively employed in the smelting and manufacturing of iron. On Oil and Scrubgrass creeks, on the river, near Lawrenceburgh, and in Armstrong county, near Kittanning, are already erected furnaces, which produce large quantities of good iron, at cheaper rates than it can be made in any other part of Pennsylvania, and which always finds an immediate and most profitable market at Pittsburgh. Other works of this kind are projected, and with every prospect of successful execution.

The country through which the Allegheny and its branches pass, is peculiarly fertile and salubrious. The counties of Erie, Crawford, Venango, and Armstrong, contain as large, if not a larger portion of arable land, than any other part of the state: and the New-York market, by ascending the river, the Pittsburgh and Western markets, by descending, are open at the election of the inhabitants of those counties. Upon the Conemaugh, the parent stream of the Kiskeminitas, and along the sides of the Allegheny river, rich salt springs are every where found.

The lands which are within the basin of the Allegheny, amount to 6,267,400 acres.

The capacity of the Allegheny for improvement, is as great as that of any river in Pennsylvania. It has no precipitous falls; it has no large or rugged rocks to render its navigation dangerous, and which would create difficulties in clearing its bed. It has at all times, a sufficient quantity of water, which if thrown together by dams, would furnish deep and not rapid channels; materials for its improvement abound every where.—These circumstances, together with the number of its deep and extensive pools, will render the cost of the work which would make a steam-boat navigation on the Allegheny to Warren, very inconsiderable. Part of the river has been examined by the Engineers of the United States; and it would not be an extravagant as to calculation, in saying, that this work, under the charge of judicious and competent persons, would not cost beyond the sum of $400,000.

The Monongahela, at Pittsburgh, is about 1400 feet in breadth, over which there is a bridge thrown from Smithfield street, of 8 arches of 187 feet span. This river rises in the Laurel mountains, in Harrison county, Virginia, and after pursuing a north-eastwardly course of about 160 miles, enters Pennsylvania, when it immediately wheels to the west, and continues that course, generally, until its junction with the Allegheny. It is a dull and sluggish stream, and owing to the mud and loam of its bed and banks, the water is dark and turbid. It is navigable with keel-boats, almost at all seasons, as far as Brownsville, which is about 60 miles above Pittsburgh; but during high water, boats may ascend 70 or 80 miles further. The principal tributaries of the Monongahela, are the East Branch, Cheat river, and the Youghiogany. The first enters in the county in which the Monongahela originates; the second, about 4 miles below the Pennsylvania line, and the third, 15 miles above Pittsburgh. They all take their rise in the Great Backbone mountain; are rapid and crooked streams, and after heavy rains or great thaws, send down immense bodies of water. The Monongahela, from its source downwards, presents about 18 towns and villages—the most important of which, are Morgantown, and Clarksburgh, in Virginia, and Brownsville, in Pennsylvania. The latter place is situated on the south-east bank of the river, where it is crossed by the national road. It is in Fayette county, and although not the capital, is incorporated. Brownsville is one of the most important and thriving towns in the western part of the state; it was laid out in 1785, but its prosperity, in a great measure, has been confined to later years. It carries on a considerable trade, and has several manufactories. Several steam-boats have been built here, and annually, about 150 keel and flat boats are sent to Pittsburgh, where they are generally sold. The staple commodities of the place, and surrounding country, are whiskey, flour, glass, iron, cider, grain, and produce of all kinds, the principal part of which finds a market at Pittsburgh. The population of Brownsville are highly enterprizing and industrious, and is in number, about 1500; in the town there are 250 houses, about 12 stores, and 6 or 8 public inns. The Mononga-hela, after leaving Harrison, passes through Monongalia county, and divides Greene from Fayette, and part of Washington from Westmoreland and Allegheny; is free from islands, but has numerous bars and shoals.

The country bordering on the river, is broken and une-ven, " presenting in some parts, deep and narrow ravines; in others, large flats of meadow lands, and not unfrequent-ly, surfaces composed entirely of rock; the soil is conse-quently, of various qualities; many parts are barren and unproductive; but much good land, and fine timber fre-quently occur." In the hilly regions, coal and iron abound in plenty.

It has not been until within a few years since, that the Monongahela, or any of its intersecting streams, have ap-peared to excite any interest in regard to their localities, and it is only since those great and important questions of internal improvement, by canals, have been agitated, that the natural resources of Pennsylvania have been consult-ed. Heretofore, the south-eastern part of our state, and that part of Maryland adjoining, were considered of little importance; their hilly and mountainous aspect, with which much barrenness and sterility are always identified, rendered them scarcely worthy of geographical or scien-tific research. But now, as the lever of actual observa-tion has removed many doubts and prejudices, relative to these long forgotten hills and vallies, it is discovered that they contain those means and advantages which may ren-der their meanest spots useful and valuable. In the con-templated connection of the Potomac and Ohio, the tract of country just mentioned, is that through which the line of communication must be laid, and the streams of Cheat and Youghiogany rivers are mentioned as the principal mediums through one or the other which the great work will be completed, from the dividing ridge. Cheat river, however, is said to present the greatest facilities of the two, as having fewer natural obstructions, and approach-ing the nearest to the eastern section. The route to be pursued up this stream will continue from its mouth about 24 miles to Dunkard's Bottom, where it is intersected by Muddy creek; thence by Muddy creek to the Pine swamp, where it originates; thence across into the Muddy creek branch of the Youghiogany, which also arises in the same swamp; thence down this stream to the Youghiogany river, crossing which, it enters Deep creek valley, holding a powerful stream of that name, which produces vast quantities of water; the route then continues up this valley and the north fork of the creek, to the dividing ridge, at a point where it would be nearest and most convenient to connect it, by a tunnel, with the Crab tree fork of Savage river, which empties into the Potomac 33 miles above Cumberland. The whole distance from the dividing ridge to the Monongahela river, is 53 miles; that from the summit level to the mouth of Savage river, on the Potomac, is 13 miles; making the whole distance between the rivers, to be connected, about 66 miles. Of Cheat river, there is only 12 miles declared navigable by law; the balance of its course to Muddy creek, is full of rapids and falls, one of which descends 30 feet in a mile; this would require locks; the others would admit of a sluice navigation. There are no towns or villages on Cheat river, and but few settlements, consequently, the country is wild, and in a state of nature.

Taking the Youghiogany, there are two routes that present themselves as practicable; one, by following the course of that stream to Castleman's river, by which, and a tunnel through the ridge, it might be connected with Wills' creek, a tributary of the Potomac, flowing in near Cumberland; the other, by following the Youghiogany to Deep creek, and then striking into the line of the Cheat river route, as before mentioned. Upon these routes, however, says Mr. Shriver, an able and practical engineer, many formidable obstacles to the formation of a canal will be found, although, none of which are of an insuperable nature. In pursuing the ravine of the Youghiogany, the canal would have to cross it frequently, or be carried in many places, along rocky and precipitous banks. On more than one half the distance there is, nevertheless, highly favourable ground for canalling.

The Youghiogany may be ascended in boats about 40 miles, to Connelsville, which may be termed as the *cognoscentii* of Wheeling are pleased to say of their beautiful *strip* of houses, *the head of navigation*. The town is situated on the west bank, in Fayette county, and has a population of about 500. There are in the neighbourhood, forges, and furnaces, mills, etc. from which great quantities of metal, flour and other articles are brought to the Pittsburgh market. 2*

There are several other villages on the Youghiogany but they are, as yet, of little importance.

The face of the country here, as is remarked by Mr. Shriver, is rugged and broken, but in many places, there are limestone districts, and sugar-tree lands of great fertility; a great part them, although in a mountainous region, lie handsome for cultivation.

The glades, or natural meadow lands, which may be considered as the most remarkable, as well as the most interesting feature in this tract of country, are found extended, as it were, on the very summit of the dividing mountains, many miles in every direction. The Youghiogany glade extends from the mouth of that river to the source of the Little Youghiogany creek. The hills surrounding this glade are generally covered with a thin growth of white-oak; others are entirely bald. At the head of the branches of the stream, stand several of these hills possessing bold, well defined, and beautiful forms, presenting, in contrast with the timber-clad hills of the mountains, interesting appearances of much singularity.

Of minerals, iron may be considered as the most prominent. Stone-coal has also been found on the banks of the Youghiogany, of excellent quality.

There are many natural curiosities and mineral springs, a description of which, time prevents us from giving.

Having digressed considerably up the tributaries of the Monongahela, we shall now return to that stream, at the mouth of the Youghiogany; after passing this river, it continues gently to widen, as it winds its serpentine way through the undulating hills; when having proceeded about 6 miles, the first object that occurs worthy of notice, is a large shoal or ripple extending across the river, called BRADDOCK'S FORDING; bearing the name of that unfortunate officer, who, over this rapid, led a brave and efficient army to destruction. The battle ground is a short distance below, on the right; but the advantages or disadvantages of either army, in that bloody encounter, cannot now be particularly ascertained; the ravine where the French and Indians formed their fatal ambuscade, and the surrounding woods that concealed the red allies of France, having been cleared and enclosed, forming part of a large and capacious farm, which is now the elegant and hospitable residence of George Wallace, Esq. The place presents no memento of that disastrous event, but the crumbling bones of the unfortunate victims which, unburied, lie strewed and bleaching in the summer sun—the husband-man passes over them with his plough and his harrow, un-conscious, perhaps, that he is crushing into dust all that remains of a hero; and in the harvest time, fields of yellow grain wave over the spot enriched by the blood of a thou-sand brave men.   Poor Braddock himself, in this fatal contest, received a mortal wound, and died a few days afterwards.   His body was interred a few miles east of Uniontown, in the middle of the road, to prevent the sa-vages from discovering it.   "The name of Braddock," says a modern writer, "has not been cherished by his countrymen, and no attempt has been made to rescue his fame from obloquy—perhaps, because no plausible ground of vindication exists; but every feeling mind must deplore the premature death of a brave, though obstinate leader, and the sacrifice of a gallant army.   There is nothing more arbitrary than the meed of applause or opprobium, bestowed upon the soldiers toils; success being too gener-ally the test of military merit.   We are therefore, chari-tably disposed towards military miscarriages, and to ven-erate the shades of the fallen brave, although they may have fallen unwisely.   He who gives his life to his coun-try, gives his all, and having thus proved the sincerity of his patriotism, leaves his reputation to posterity, with a sacred and imposing claim upon their candour.   In the tempest of that day which consigned Braddock to an un-honoured grave, the genius of Washington dawned with a lustre which gave promise of its future greatness, and the American reveres the spot which has been hallowed by the illustrious presence and gallant deeds of the father of his country."

Soon after leaving the fording, commence those bars, which are found in the Monongahela, from time to time, until its junction with the Allegheny.   The bar at Pitts-burgh, is about two miles in length, and from 100 to 250 yards in breadth, and consists entirely of fine sand. The channel is on the side next the city, which, at the very lowest stage of water, affords a depth of from 5 to 12 feet.   The shipping business is all done on the Mo-nongahela, as the wharves are built upon it, and as the Allegheny shore is devoted to lumber rafts, iron and salt. As all the wharfage to be received for some years, will be applied to the improvement of the beach of the Monongahela, it is to be presumed that there will be a handsome and extensive quay constructed in a short time.

Connected with Pittsburgh, and as a component part of the objects to be taken into view in this work, is the COUNTY OF ALLEGHENY, in which the city is situated. It is bounded on the east and south, by Westmoreland, and Washington; and on the north and west, by Butler and Beaver. Its length is 28, and its breadth 27 miles, and contains 754 square miles. The population was,

In 1800	15,087
1810	25,317
1820	34,921
1826, about	40,300

giving about 53 to every square mile.

The surrounding country is very hilly, and a considerable portion of the land very sterile, particularly that part adjoining Butler. The best lands lie along, and adjacent the rivers. The upland, however, is very fine in many places, producing all the necessaries of life, as well for transportation as home consumption, in abundance, and is crowned with the finest timber. The bottoms are generally all cleared, and are devoted principally to corn, owing to their great fertility. The finest part of the county may be said to lie south of the Monongahela, and west of the Ohio, extending from Chartiers creek; and that portion lying above the Youghiogany, commonly called the "Forks of Yough." The vallies are few and very narrow, just admitting the passage of some wandering stream, and occasionally a strip of meadow. Beside the villages heretofore spoken of, there are several others in the county: Elizabethtown, on the Monongahela, 15 miles from Pittsburgh; M'Keesport, at the mouth of the Youghiogany; East Liberty, on the Philadelphia turnpike; Wilkinsburgh, on the same; Noblesburgh, Perrysville, &c. They are all small places, and do not present any thing worthy of remark. Of the business, proceeds of agricultural labours, &c. of the county, we shall speak under another head.

Having now concluded our topographical observations, we shall proceed to say something of the early history of Pittsburgh, and its subsequent vicissitudes.

HISTORICAL.

SCARCE half a century is gone by, since Pittsburgh was an inconsiderable hamlet, destitute of all the appearances which indicate the presence of wealth or comfort, and valuable only as a frontier military defence against the inroads of the savages or the French. Few of the ancient men, who were the chroniclers of adventures and sufferings, of which this portion of Pennsylvania was the scene, now survive. Yet, there are some, who bear in distinct recollection the time of peril and dismay, when the cruelties of the aborigines, and the ambition of their instigators and allies, rendered Pittsburgh unsafe as a permanent residence. The appalling yell of the savage, as he started from his ambush, or witnessed the agonies of his burning prisoner, was but a few years since, heard where this prosperous and populous city now attracts the attention of the stranger, as the bustling workshop of the west. Then, a few daring traders, of the blood of the whites, and red men, almost as civilized as themselves, brought to the little store of the merchant, the furs and peltry, which constituted the principal domestic articles of traffic. The solitary canoe was seen gliding along the Allegheny, or moored at the beach, laden with the products of the chase, to be exchanged for the rude materials of clothing, and the munitions of warfare or of hunting.

These circumstances and events, which are the subject of tradition among most of us, and are remembered by so few who saw them, and participated in them, may be without interest for those who are, and always have been distant from the scene where they were witnessed and done. The gradual, or rapid advance of men or communities, from the first humble state of existence to the acquisition of wealth and consequence, is, indeed, but the ordinary result of human effort and perseverance, judiciously directed, and often of long duration. They should not enter into the narrative of general history; nor do they attract intense or common observation. But, to those who were born or have long resided, where they transpired, they must be interesting as the subject-matter of the domestic legends which have beguiled the evenings of their childhood, or been listened to with eager attention, in more advanced life. They are part of the history of the western country, serving to display the intrepid character of its early inhabitants, and will, therefore, be heard with pleasure, by those among us, who look with a kindling eye on the page which records the doings and sufferings of their forefathers or predecessors.

Pittsburgh, from its situation, at the head of the Ohio, and at the confluence of the two rivers which form that stream, was probably first noticed for its military rather than its commercial advantages. The early French and English settlers of this country, were engaged in continual wars with each other, and with the natives, in the course of which, the former determined to establish a chain of posts from Canada to Louisiana. One of the most important of these, was Fort Du Quesne, situated at this point. It did not escape the military eye of Washington, when he visited this country, several years before the revolution, on a mission from the governor of Virginia; and in his despatches he speaks of its importance with a prophetic spirit. During the struggle, which is commonly called Braddock's war, fort Du Quesne changed masters, and the English, abandoning the original work, which was probably a mere stockade, built a more regular fortification on a site immediately adjoining, which they named fort Pitt, in honor of the Earl of Chatham. This post, erected on a low point of land, and commanded by hills on every side, would appear to a soldier of the present day, to have been useless; nor can the reasons of its original establishment, and subsequent importance, be ascertained, without recurring to the events of that early period. As a place of deposit for military stores, no other spot could have been so eligible, as there is none from which they could be distributed with equal celerity, over so large an extent of country. Nor was its situation with regard to defence, so desperate as we might first imagine. It is to be recollected, that in those days there was little or no artillery west of the mountains, and that it was considered as almost impossible to cross the rugged cliffs of the Allegheny ridge with a carriage of any description. There was little reason, therefore, to apprehend that any ordnance would be brought to storm the ramparts of fort Pitt. But, notwithstanding this imagined security, the works, of which there are extensive ruins, seem to have been built after the usual fashion of that time. A bomb-proof magazine is still extant, but considerably dilapidated. They are said to have been built by Lord Stanwin, and cost the British government 60,000 pounds sterling. As it would seem by placing the fort at this exposed spot, that an attack by artillery was not apprehended, and as, if such an attack had been made, resistance would have been in vain, it is difficult to conceive what could have been the motives of the builders to give it such strength and regularity. We must either suppose that their military habits prevailed over the dictates of prudence, or that they intended to impress their Indian neighbours with an exalted opinion of their security and power. Shortly after the English took possession, the Indian traders built a row of fine buildings on the margin of the Allegheny, but their foundations were sapped by the encroachments of the river, and they fell; no vestiges of them now remain. About the year 1760, a small town was built near fort Pitt, which contained about two hundred souls; but on the breaking out of the Indian war in 1763, the inhabitants were obliged to retire into the fort for several months, during which time it was closely invested by the savages. Being destitute of the means of making regular approaches, the Indians took post on the banks of the adjacent rivers, and blockaded it so effectually that they cut off all communication from without. The commander of the British forces in America, sensible, from the situation of the place, that it would be a principle object of savage fury, despatched Col. Bonquet with a large quantity of provisions and military stores, under a strong escort, to the relief of the garrison. On the 5th of August, the detachment arrived at fort Ligonier. In order to facilitate their march, the wagons and heavy baggage were left there, whilst the Colonel proceeded with the troops, and about 250 barrels of flour on pack-horses. The Indians having intelligence of their approach, abandoned the blockade of fort Pitt to attack them on their march. On the night of the 10th of August, when Bonquet had advanced within 35 miles of Pittsburgh, and while his troops were refreshing themselves after a fatiguing march, his advanced guard was suddenly attacked; but being speedily reinforced, the savages were repulsed and pur-

sued a considerable way. On the following morning they
returned and attacked the camp under an incessant fire.
It was in vain for the British to repel them, because when
pressed they retired, but returned with redoubled ardour.
The condition of the detachment was truly deplorable;
galled by the fire of the Indians, and faint and dispirited·
through a total want of water, and three-fourths of their
camp surrounded. Thus situated, Captain Barret, who
commanded a company of provincial riflemen, proposed to
Col. Bonquet to lead out two companies privately through
a narrow defile, in the only quarter from which they were
not assailed. The plan was adopted, and succeeded—
the Indians receiving a heavy fire in their rear, conceived
it to be a reinforcement from fort Pitt, and immediately
fled. The detachment then continued its march, and in
four days afterwards arrived at the fort, which they found
almost reduced to extremity.

Fort Du Quesne was built about the year 1753, and was
held in quiet possession by the French until 1758, when
General Forbes was sent by the British government to cap-
ture and destroy it. The general, however, considering
the reduction of the fort a matter of easy accomplishment,
did not think worth while to march thither with the whole
of his army, but despatched Colonel Grant, a gallant officer, with about 800 Highlanders, to surprise the garrison.
The Colonel and his party arrived in the evening at the
height which now bears his name, intending early the succeeding morning to plant the British flag on the ramparts
of the French fortress. The morning found him ready for
action, and confident of success—but elated by the impunity which had thus far attended his enterprize, or despi-
sing his inactive foe, who seemed already within his grasp,
in a moment of incaution he ordered his musicians to
sound the *reveille.* As the martial sounds stole along the
hills, calling forth their sleeping echoes, the brave Scots
might have fancied themselves in that far awa' land which
a Scotsman never forgets—but, alas! Those bugle blasts
which aroused their hearts to enthusiasm, were the last
they were destined to hear. The French and Indians,
thus informed by their enemy of his approach, sallied privately from the fort, possessed themselves of the hills in
the rear of Grant, and of the ·surrounding coverts, and
rushing in upon the unsuspecting Scots, cut them in pieces.

General Forbes, on hearing the fate Col. Grant, and his detachment, immediately proceeded to Pittsburgh with the remainder of the army; but on his arrival, he found the fort evacuated, and he entered it unmolested.

It would be an endless task to point out all those spots around Pittsburgh which have been rendered interesting by the events of the days long past; they are endeared to the Pennsylvanian by many fond associations. It is not the vales and streams that delight merely by their intrinsic beauty, but every neighbouring eminence and winding glade has been the scene of hardy achievements. This was one of the first points selected by those who commenced the work of civilization in the Western Country. Here all the difficulties of a new settlement; the horrors of Indian warfare, and the bereavements of an isolated society, cut off from assistance, and almost from intercourse, were encountered to the fullest extent. The Allegheny ridge then presented a formidable barrier, and they who passed it found themselves in a new world, where they must defend themselves or perish. The first settlers therefore, waged continual war—they fought *pro aris et focis*—for life, and all that makes life dear. But these wars were distinguished only by acts of individual prowess, and produced none of those great events which affect national fame or greatness, and which it is the province of the historian to record. They will, therefore, find no place in the annals of our country. Yet, the day will surely come, when the poet and the novelist will traverse these regions in quest of traditionary lore, will listen with eagerness to the tales of hoary headed sires, and laboriously glean the frail and mutilated memorials of the doings of other days. Then will the gallant men who have smoothed our path, and conquered for us the country of which we are now so proud, find a place, if not with better men, at least with the Rodericks and Rob Roys of fiction.

After Fort Pitt came into possession of the Americans, it was occupied for a short time, and then became one of the manors of the Penn family. In 1765, Pittsburgh was regularly laid out as a town, including the garrison—but in 1784, as we have stated in our topographical remarks, it was again located on a different plan.—The fort being removed about half a mile up the Allegheny, where a picket work, block house and barracks were erected, called "Fort

Fayette." This fort was occupied by the United States' troops until the building of the Arsenal at Lawrenceville.

The increase of Pittsburgh was not rapid until the year 1793, in consequence of the wars, which also impeded the growth and extension of the neighbouring settlements. The Western Insurrection, more generally known as the "Whiskey war," once more made the town the scene of trouble and commotion; and we regret that our limits will not permit us to give any of the interesting incidents that occurred during that far famed opposition to an obnoxious measure of government. However, it is said that this insurrection, by throwing into circulation a good deal of the public money, gave to Pittsburgh a new and reviving impulse, it having since that time progressed very rapidly.

Twenty-five years ago, when this settlement was in its infancy, legal science flourished with a vigor unusual in rude societies. The bench and the bar presented a galaxy of eloquence and learning. Judge ADDISON, who first presided in this circuit under the present system, possessed a fine mind and great attainments. He was an accomplished scholar, deeply versed in every branch of classical learning. In law and theology he was great—but although he explored the depths of science with unwearied assiduity, he could sport in the sunbeams of literature, and cull with nice discrimination, the flowers of poesy. He assumed his judicial authority under many perplexing circumstances. The country was new, and the people factious—the bar was undisciplined, and the rules of practice vague—the judiciary system had been newly modelled, and was now to be tested; its excellence to be proved, and its defects to be discovered—and while an unusal weight of responsibility thus devolved upon the judge, the novelty of his situation must often have left him without precedents to govern his decisions. These circumstances would have daunted a man of less firmness than Judge Addison, but his mind possessed an energetic vigor which opposition could not subdue nor difficulty embarrass. His decisions were so uniformly correct, that few of them have been reversed; they have been published, together with a number of charges delivered to grand juries, and the volume is in high repute among the lawyers of Pennsylvania. We should be happy to be able to add that this distinguished man was rewarded for his services, and permitted to be useful as long as he continued to be honoured. But it was not so. He became obnoxious to a dominant faction; was impeached, condemned, and hurled from a seat to which he had given dignity, for an act which was probably right, but which, if wrong, was not *dishonourable* or *corrupt.* Such are the effects of party spirit—its venom, like a poisonous miasm, pervades the whole atmosphere in which it is generated, and creates a pestilence which sweeps worth and worthlessness to a common grave.

This gentleman was succeeded by Judge ROBERTS, an excellent lawyer, and a man of great integrity and knowledge, who wanted only the energy of his predecessor. He had firmness enough to be always upright, nor could he be swayed from an honest conviction, or intimidated in discharge of the duties of his office; but he was too mild to enforce a rigid discipline in his court, and too passive for the despatch of business. He could neither be biassed nor alarmed—but he had too much of the "milk of human kindness" in his nature, and loved mankind too well to be a judge of human actions. The hall of justice brings together all the elements of discord—the angry passions are roused—turbulent spirits are brought into contact—life, fortune and character are at stake—hopes and fears are awakened—crime, folly and misfortune are disclosed—the veil of secrecy is torn from the sorrows of the heart, and the scenes of the fire-side—and the man who can gaze on such a scene with a steady eye, and decide with collected promptness, must have a very firm or a very cold heart. The gentleman of whom we are speaking, had no coldheartedness in his composition; his sympathies were easily awakened, and his was a heart of too much candour and generosity to conceal, or be ashamed of an honourable impulse. Yet his mind possessed great vigor and clearness, and he was universally esteemed, as well for his good sense and attainments, as for his uprightness and amiability. They who knew him best will always remember him with kindness, and his decisions will be respected when none of us shall be left who knew his virtues. He is sometime deceased.

Judge WILKINS, who succeeded judge Roberts, but who is now presiding over the Western District court of Pennsylvania, has long been a prominent man. As an advocate, he was among the foremost, and as a citizen has always been conspicuous. His public spirit and capacity for business, have thrown him into a multitude of offices. He presided for many years over one of the branches of the corporation; has represented his county in the legislature; was president of the Pittsburgh Bank, and of several companies inc rporated for the purpose of internal improvement. Judge Wilkins has brought to the bench an active mind, much legal experience and an intimate knowledge. of the practice of courts; but as he is still on the stage, we must not be his biographer.

There were at the bar in the olden time, many illustrious pillars of the law—STEELE SEMPLE, long since deceased, a man of stupendous genius, spoken of by his cotemporaries, as a prodigy of eloquence and legal attainment:—JAMES ROSS, who is still practicing, and very generally known as a great statesman and eminent advocate—who for depth of thought, beauty of language, and dignity of manners, has scarcely an equal: WOODS, COLLINS, CAMPBELL and MOUNTAIN would have shone at any bar. HENRY BALDWIN, who is still on the stage, an eminent lawyer; a rough, but powerful and acute speaker—as a member of congress, he was very conspicuous, as the chairman of the committee on Domestic Manufactures, and as the author and able advocate of the celebrated tariff bill.

The bar of Pittsburgh, in modern times, presents a list of followers of the law, of considerable length; but as to talents, with a few exceptions, they bear no comparison to those who flourished in those days to which we have heretofore alluded. The greater part of the members of this period are young men, the ambition of some of whom soared no higher than to have the respectable title of "Attorney and Counsellor at law" tacked to their natural cognomen; intending afterwards, to leave the acquirement of legal knowledge, which is only to be obtained by deep study and intense application, to the drudgery of a fugitive practice. Among the exceptions which we make, the names of WALTER FORWARD and RICHARD BIDDLE may be mentioned. These are gentlemen of sterling talents, and great legal attainments. While we are on this subject, we cannot help mentioning, how much we deprecate the roguery of many parents of the present time, in relation to the views they entertain of the future destinies of their children. Scarce has the citizen or mechanic acquired a little competency, than his son (if he has one) is destined to become a candidate for civic honors—a follower of Hippocrates, or a novitiate for holy orders.—We say *roguery*, because by devoting these youths to those professions, the mechanic's shop is often cheated out of many an able bodied man, who in the line of his father's business might have done credit to the manufacturing interests of his country; whereas on the other hand, in pursuing the studies necessary to make a lawyer, a doctor, or a minister, how many are there, who becoming sensible of their incapacity to arrive at eminence, or even a respectable mediocrity, retire in disgust, and lead a life of uselessness, if not of dissipation. Or if there are any who betray some scintillations of uncommon genius, they are often so honied over by the fulsome flattery of friends and relations; and *indulgence*, that bane of our early years, is so liberally meted out, that unless the object of these attentions possesses a mind of unusual strength, he becomes at once the victim of vanity, and the train of vices that too generally follow. Far be it from us to say, who are mechanics ourselves and proud of the appellation, that the sons of professional men, are less thick-skulled or possess greater capabilities than those of mechanics, or that the former are less liable to disgrace and worthlessness than the latter. No; we only wish to shew how ridiculous and absurd it is, that every man who follows a laborious occupation, by which he has accumulated considerable wealth, should consider his son too good to pursue that business to which his life had been devoted.

But to return—as we have dwelt at some length on those, whose legal and classic knowledge once shed lustre o'er the land, we must not forget those who have rendered Pittsburgh conspicuous for its hospitality in the ancient time, and we cannot but regret that those good old times of liberal feeling and social intercourse have gone by, and given way to those cold and heartless formalities that distinguish the present day. That there are virtues in refinement, no one will presume to doubt—but it has its excesses. *That* refinement which compels a stranger, on his introduction, when he pulls off his hat with one hand, to thrust out his pedigree with the other, while the whispering interrogatories of "who is he," "what is he" and "what is he worth," are echoed from the cellar to the garret with the lightnings' rapidity, is as ridiculous as it is contemptible. And *that* refinement which excludes purity and worth from the assemblies of the rich, because their possessor is poor, or because he is not even remotely al-

3 *

lied to some distinguished family, is despicable, as creating
dictinctions altogether foreign to that republican simplicity
which should characterize an American people. When
Pittsburgh was a village, the better and kindlier feelings
predominated, unclouded by fashionable doubts and refined
prejudices, and to point out where those virtues existed,
we need but mention the habitations of Gen. O'Hara, Gen.
Neville and Gen. Wilkins, with many others. Their
homes were the dwelling places of genuine hospitality—
where the decent stranger, uninterrogated, was welcomed
to the festive and social board, and where the poor received in abundance those necessaries which the charity of
liberal hands, and the benevolence of generous hearts bestowed. These gentlemen have, some time since, gone to
"that bourne whence no traveller returns;" but their
memories will long be cherished by those who knew them.
The mantle of their generosity has fallen on but few.

In regard to the manufacturing and commercial interests
of Pittsburgh, the year Eighteen hundred and twenty-six
presents the most ample proof of their prosperity. The
census too, of the year, gives an astonishing increase of
population, which indicates in itself the progress of business,
and gives cause of much congratulation. Whatever may
have been the greatness of Pittsburgh in times past, and
whatever may have been those subsequent failures which
depressed her citizens, and shut up their manufactories,
we feel assured that her present prosperous concerns are
founded on a solid basis; that they have not been entered
into prematurely; nor are they put into operation without
those resources which are necessary to carry them on.
The numerous monied institutions which formerly existed,
and which threw into circulation through promiscuous and
afterwards unfortunate borrowers, such heaps of worthless
paper currency, have long since gone down. The few
stable institutions of that kind of the present day, keep a
circulating medium of credit and usefulness, and their judicious loans will always be serviceable without producing
the fatal effects that marked similar transactions in our
former seemingly prosperous periods.

In short, with Pittsburgh there are few places that can
compete. If her citizens are just to themselves; if they
keep a steady eye on their own interests, by fostering their
resources, opening the channels of their commerce, and
by being satisfied with a liberal profit on their manufacturing and trading commodities, she must and will be great,

SALUBRITY.

Communicated by Dr. William H. Denny.

OF all the great western towns, Pittsburgh is the farthest removed from the baneful exhalations of the swampy margin of the Mississippi, and accordingly enjoys a greater exemption from those diseases, which during the summer and autumn, prevail even as high up as Cincinnati. Surrounded too, by hills and cultivated lands, and free from stagnant water, there are no local sources of disease. The smoke of bituminous coal is anti-miasmatic. It is sulphurous and antiseptic, and hence it is, perhaps, that no putrid disease has ever been known to spread in the place. Strangers with weak lungs, for a while, find their coughs aggravated by the smoke; but nevertheless, asthmatic patients have found relief in breathing it. The prevailing complaints are those which characterize the healthiest situations of the same latitude elsewhere in America—in winter, pneumonia and sore throat, and in summer, bilious affections. The goitre, or swelled neck, has disappeared; the few cases which formerly excited the apprehensions of the stranger, no longer exist to gratify his curiosity. In comparison with the eastern cities, there is much less pulmonary consumption; less scrofula, and less disease of the skin. There is scarcely any ague and fever, and no yellow fever. In comparison with the western cities, including Cincinnati, there is less bilious fever; less ague and fever, and less cholera infantum, or the summer complaint of children. We are the intermediate link of disease, as well as of commerce. We have less hepatic disease than the west, and less pulmonic disease than the east.

The abundance, cheapness, and consequent general and even profuse use of the best fuel, is certainly one great cause of our superior healthfulness. The low fevers so prevalent in the large cities, among the poor, during a hard winter, and the ague so common in wet seasons, in the eastern counties of the state, where wood is scarce, are here in a great degree avoided by the universal practice of

keeping good coal fires late in the spring, and early in the
autumn, and indeed at all seasons when .the weather is
damp or inclement.

Our exemption from the ague, and epidemic dysenteries,
in comparison with the settlements in the lower counties,
and the eastern vallies, may be accounted for also, in part,
by the scarcity of mill-dams and stagnant water, in a
county where in the summer, milling for the most part, is
done by steam, and where the mill streams generally dry
up at the season most likely to produce disease.

Dyspepsia, and chronic affections of the liver, are becoming more common, and the diseases of intemperance
are increasing. Our great manufacturing establishments
may be expected, in the course of time, to add to the bills
of infirmity; but, probably, never to the extent that similar pursuits have produced in Europe. Our youth are not
so early introduced into factories; the confinement is not
so great; the food is more nutricious; but few dwell in
cellars or work in crowded apartments, and none labour
under the continual apprehension of being, by the fluctua-
ations of trade, thrown out of employment, and wanting
bread.

In the whole, with regard to the health of Pittsburgh,
and indeed, of the whole western section of Pennsylvania,
it may be said, that no part of the United States is more
healthy, and that the greater part will bear no comparison
with it in point of salubrity.

CORPORATION, COUNCILS, &c.

By an act of the General Assembly, passed the 18th of March, 1816, Pittsburgh was incorporated into a city and body politic, by the name and style of the "Mayor, Aldermen and Citizens of Pittsburgh." The legislative powers of the corporation, are vested in fifteen persons, who as a body, are called the *Common Council;* and in nine persons, who are called the *Select Council.* Their election takes place annually on the first Tuesday of January. The members of the Select Council are divided into three classes. The seats of the first class are vacated at the expiration of the first year—the second class at the expiration of the second year—and the third class at the expiraof the third year, so that one third may be chosen every year. No person who is an alderman, or who holds an office of trust or profit under this commonwealth, or under the ordinances of the councils, (the emoluments whereof are paid out of the city treasury) can be competent to serve as a select or common council man. The powers and authorities of the corporation extend to the passage of such laws and ordinances as may be necessary for the safety, convenience and good government of the city; and to lay and collect fines and penalties for the breach of them. They have also the power to regulate the market; fix the assize of bread; erect wharves and collect wharfage; regulate the landing of all kinds of water craft, and prevent every description of animals from running at large. They have the power to levy taxes on all species of property that may be subject to taxation for county purposes. They have also the right to regulate or prohibit all kinds of shows in the city, and to license as many brokers as may be necessary. In short, they are vested with all the powers and privileges of the corporation of the city of Philadelphia.

During the Session of 1816–17, a supplement to the act of incorporation was passed.—This supplement was enacted, for increasing the judiciary powers of the mayor's court;

to give to the aldermen the same powers and jurisdiction as
a justice of the peace; to fix the recorder's salary; to au-
thorise the issuing of writs of Habeas Corpus, &c. Upon this
bill being presented to Mr. Snyder, the then governor,
for approval, he refused his sanction, and returned it with
objections; however it was afterwards agreed to by two
thirds of each house and became a law.

The municipal officers of the city, consist of a Mayor,
Recorder, twelve Aldermen, Treasurer, Weighmaster of
markets, Assessor, Collector, Weighmaster of Hay, three
Board Measurers, Salt Inspector, Inspector of Pot and
Pearl ashes, Tobacco Inspector, three Street Regulators, Street Commissioner, Clerk of the market, High
Constable, and four city Constables. The mayor must be,
at the time of his nomination, one of the twelve aldermen,
and is elected by the councils conjointly assembled, on the
second Tuesday of January, annually. The Recorder and
Aldermen hold their offices by appointment from the Executive of the state, and continue in the same during good
behaviour. The other officers execpt the Street Commissioner and four Constables, who are chosen by the mayor,
are in the gift of the councils, and are by them chosen,
viva voce, on the same day with the mayor.

Municipal Court, &c.

The judicial powers of the corporation are vested in the
Mayor, Recorder and Aldermen, or any four of them;
(whereof the Mayor or Recorder for the time being shall be
one) they have the privilege and authority to hold and
keep a court of record within the city four times in each
year—then to hear and determine all forgeries, perjuries,
larcenies, assaults and batteries, riots, routs, and unlawful
assemblies—and all other offences which shall be committed
within the city, and which would be cognizable in any
court of Quarter Sessions in Pennsylvania; and to sentence
to punishment, all persons who may be convicted of such
offences.

In all cases determined in this court, when a party may
feel aggrieved by any of its judgments, he or she may sue
out and obtain a writ of error to the Supreme court in the

same manner as in the Common pleas.   The Recorder has
full power to issue writs of *Habeas Corpus* in all cases, and
release thereon as fully as Judges of other courts.   Of the
Mayor's court the Mayor is the presiding officer, but the
Recorder is the legal organ, as through him the opinions
of the court are expressed.

If there were any benefits resulting to our citizens from
the incorporation of Pittsburgh into a city, the establishment
of a city court, was certainly among the most prominent.
By it, the regular Quarter Sessions were relieved of an immense mass of trifling and unimportant cases, which for
years, with increasing numbers were, if not impeding the
regular stream of justice, preventing the consummation of
many civil suits of much moment, by causing great delays.
Two or three days are now devoted to Quarter Sesson business, which used to occupy six or seven. In looking at our
civil and criminal courts they present a degree of litigation,
that to a church-going people, as we have been styled, is not
very creditable, and it is much to be regretted that in the
latter court, there is so much countenance given to pet-
ty and trivial prosecutions, by those who have it in their
power to quash or prevent them. Of assaults and batteries
there appears to be no decrease; mankind are generally
disposed to revenge either by force or law.—Thus, if a
fellow insults another, and for his impertinence receives a
blow or a kick, and has not courage enough to make good
his words, and turns coward, he immediately seeks ven-
geance through the glorious uncertainty of the law, by fly-
ing to a Justices' office. The officer seldom interposes to
make up matters, and a suit is the result.   However,
matters of this kind might be got through with, notwithstanding the trouble given to the court and the expenses of
continuing juries, if the parties were able to pay the
costs, as by their inability the county is saddled with the
expenses of all these worthless trials. The amount of money that is paid every year by the Commissioners in cases
of this kind is enormous; and considering that the treasury
is by no mens overflowing, it ill becomes those who have
so powerful an abstract control over it, to waste the
public funds by a vain and useless, though apparently
legal attempt to administer justice.

Grand Juries have great powers in the prevention of
vexatious and litigious suits, and it is certain, that if proper
care and attention were paid by them to the character of

the evidence, its matter and manner, there would be a great decrease in the number of bills of indictment. And although the commonwealth in these cases is always plaintiff, the suit is never without a prosecutor; and when a bill is returned ignoramus, or a traverse jury find for the defendant, the person prosecuting should be made liable for the costs accrued; and this the juries have a right to determine.

Another cause of regret is, that our Mayor's court is so constantly infested with that race of persons politely termed "people of colour." It shows how liberally the law is meted out in this region. Far be it from us to say, that they should be deprived either of law or justice, in the smallest degree; but it might be considered whether by countenancing the suits of the more worthless part of them, the interests of morality were promoted, or the good order of society increased.

Corporate Authorities.

The following gentlemen compose the Corporate Authorities of the City :—

Recorder—EPHRAIM PENTLAND....Salary, $600.
Mayor—JOHN M. SNOWDEN.......Salary, $200.

Select Council.

JAMES ROSS—*President.*

JAMES ADAMS,   HARMAR DENNY,
BENJAMIN BAKEWELL,   MARTIN RAHM,
WILLIAM BLAIR,   JOHN SPEAR,
JOHN CARSON,   WILLIAM WOODS,

SAMUEL H. SCOTT, *Clerk.*

Common Council.

ALEXANDER JOHNSTON, jr.—*President.*

WILLIAM ANDERSON,   ROBERT LINDELL,
JOHN ARTHURS,   JOSEPH PATTERSON,
ANDREW BAYNE.   SAMUEL PETTIGREW,
JAMES BRYSON,   JOHN SAMPSON,
JOHN HERRON,   JOHN SHERIFF,
MALCOLM LEECH,   ROBERT STEWART
ISAAC LIGHTNER,   JAMES SPEER.

EDWARD J. ROBERTS, *Clerk.*

Meetings, last Monday of each month.

Aldermen.

JOHN DARRAGH,	ROBERT CHRISTY,
THOMAS ENOCH,	ROBERT SIMPSON,
JAMES YOUNG,	THOMAS COOPER,
JOHN M. SNOWDEN,	JOHN HANNEN,
MAGNUS M. MURRAY,	CHARLES VON BONNHORST,
MATHEW B. LOWRIE,	DENNIS S. SCULLY.

Treasurer—WILLIAM GRAHAM, jr......Salary, $150.

Weighmaster of Markets—ELIJAH TROVILLO.

Weighmaster at Hay-scales—WILLIAM EICHBAUM, sr.

Street Commissioner—WILLIAM CRAWFORD.....Salary, $200

Board Measurers.
THOMAS SCOTT, THOMAS M'KEE, and JOSEPH WELSH.

Street Regulators.
MATHIAS EVANS, ALEX. ROSEBURGH & JOHN ROBINSON.

Guager—JOSEPH BARCLAY.

Inspector of Salt—JAMES M'CRACKEN.

Wharfmaster—FLORENCE COTTER. Salary, one third of proceeds.

Inspector of Tobacco—JAMES EKIN.

Inspector of Pot and Pearl Ashes—JOHN B. GRARY.

Clerk of the Market—JAMES COOPER.

High Constable—JOHN B. GRAY.

City Constables—JOHN OSBORNE, JAMES V. GUTHRIE,
DAVID JEWELL, and SAMUEL CHRISTY.

4

APPEARANCE AND CHARACTER.

NO one who is addicted to newspaper reading, and fond of learning from the countless journals of the land, the astonishing progress of large cities, flourishing boroughs, and pleasant villages, whose eulogies are to be seen daily and weekly in typographical columns, can possibly be ignorant of the celebrity which our city has obtained as a place of all work. Its own highly favoured people, who are as tenacious of their corporate rights and municipal fame, as any New Yorker or Philadelphian ever was of his favorite town, are, by no means, sparing of their encomiums upon the wonderful natural advantages that it possesses, which are

"Familiar in their mouths as household words."

It is, indeed, not to be denied, that, for almost every kind of mechanical labour, and invention, Pittsburgh has acquired a reputation well deserved, and unsurpassed, or unrivalled by any interior town of the United States. The loud strokes of the hammer, and the lumbering of wheels, are heard within its borders, from the rising to the setting of the sun, and, when

"Winter comes to rule the varied year,"

often long after. The construction of steam boats and the fabrication of their machinery, alone, give unremitted employment to a large number of workmen. Numerous and extensive buildings are erected throughout the city, to the great annoyance of washer women and cleanly housewives, in which every process of iron manufacture is conducted. The long procession of dusky, hardy labourers, hastening to their daily tasks, or retiring from them, when the manufactory bells give note of time for toil, or its cessation, constitutes a peculiar and convincing evidence of the prosperity which Pittsburgh boasts. Upon a fortunate accumulation of the waters, the wharves, which are neither "spindled into longitude immense," nor of sufficient altitude to brave even moderate freshets, in the bustling activity, which prevails on and about them, bear no faint resemblance to the quays of a crowded maritime port. At that auspicious season, so delightful to commission merchants, freighters and dray-men, merchandize, in great quantities, and of immense value, is embarked in vessels, that complete, in a few days its transportation, which, a few years since, weeks were required to accomplish.

To a stranger, immediately preceding his entrance, the city presents an appearance sufficiently unfavourable to its character, as a place of continual residence, or even of sojourn. The atmosphere is darkened with a "sulphu-rous canopy" which nearly conceals the place from view; seems to shut it out from the light of the sun, and hangs over the valley, in which it stands, like mist exhaled from the shores of Acheron, or the smoke that hovers over

"A half unquenched volcano."

As the traveller approaches near the point of land where, he is "credibly informed," Pittsburgh is to be found, he is surprised on observing no indications, such as tall brick buildings and towering steeples stand for, of the actual entity which the place enjoys. As soon as he gains ingress to the street, that may chance to afford the first avenue for his arrival at the hotel, he looks round, with commenda-ble disgust, on the dark and melancholy aspect of men and things. Lines of low, plain brick houses, not contin-uous, but broken, ever and anon, by unseemly vacancies, or interspersed with wooden fabrics, of every size and shape, meet his disappointed eye, on this his first visit to the "Birmingham of America," the "Emporium of the West," and the "Metropolis of Western Pennsylvania." Sooth to say, he has no great reason to be much delighted, either with the detail or the *tout ensemble* of our sombre city. The streets, running at one angle here, and another there; narrow, roughly paved, filthy, beyond compare, and filled with hogs, dogs, drays and noisy children, afford a spectacle of any thing but the "sublime and beautiful." The few—no not the few, the many, large and valuable edifices, which are to be seen, are so begrimmed and mas-ked by smoke and soot, that they afford a most gloomy sight to the visiter from one of the fair cities of the east, the north, or even that miniature Philadelphia, in the west, Cincin-nati. As for lofty, glittering spires and cupolas, no such unnecessary objects, to direct the way-faring man, and embellish the city withal, are to be seen among us. The only ambitious structure that aspires to any height, within the bounds of the corporation, is the steeple of the county court house, in which is suspended a most musical bell, that threatens to bring down the daring fabric, now "tottering to its fall" with every sound of its cracked and crazy voice. This solitary spire, standing like a scathed pine in the centre of a large "clearing," around which the smoke, from heaps of burning brush, continually hovers, is no more palpable to the optics of the coming traveller, at a reasonable distance, than are the houses which inclose the little space, hight the "Public square," alias the "Diamond," where it braves the clouds in the midst. No elegant, commodious edifices are beheld, either in the "East" or "West ward" of the city. Not a single public square, appropriated to useful or ornamental purposes, is visible within the same extent of corporate limits, save and except the contracted, dirty spot of ground just mentioned; and that is so exclusively occupied by the court-house, the market-house, road wagons, carts, and drays, that but small space is left for more attractive objects. On election occasions, indeed, from twilight until midnight, the vacant part of it is held, in undisturbed possession, by a crowd of clamorous boys, and overgrown children, who alarm the vicinage, by shoutings and the display of burning balls, and blazing tar-barrels, to the great terror of all well disposed persons, and without having before their eyes the fear of the city authorities, who, for the time being, are divested of all manner of authority.

> "The man who has stood on the Acropolis,
> And look'd down o'er Attica, or he
> Who has sailed where picturesque Constantinople is,
> Or seen Tombuctoo, or has taken tea
> In small-eyed China's crockery-ware metropolis,
> Or sat amidst the bricks of Nineveh,
> May not think much of *Pittsburgh's* first appearance,
> But ask him what he thinks of it a year hence."

Something more than a year, however, would be necessary to reconcile him to the sulphurous atmosphere, and other *pleasant* qualities, which distinguish the capital of occidental Pennsylvania. Yet, strange as it may appear, to those who have, from their birth onward, inhaled the pure air of trans-montane cities, there are to be found within our city, people, and not a few, who are perfectly satisfied to make it their abiding place. Some there are too, who once, or more frequently departed from it, in great haste, and shook off the dust of their feet against it, sturdily resolved never to come within breathing distance of its abominations, who have returned to it, and are, even now, numbered among its taxable burghers. By what strange infatuation, they could have been attracted towards it—whether by an attachment to their *natale solum*—the hope of finding bank notes and substantial specie among the heaps of dust and clouds of smoke, or by some other equally powerful motive, they, alone, can pronounce. It is, most indubitably, the place of places, to gather together the "commodity," which is at once a necessary evil, the source of all mundane felicity, and the god of all mortal idolatry. Beyond, peradventure, some who reside here, in apparent contentment, merely endure their oyster-like existence, in daily expectation of amassing fortune sufficient to enable them to retire to a more pleasant city, where they may spend in refined enjoyments, the wealth which they may have acquired, with much turmoil, amid the clang of iron bars, and the suffocating fumes which they were doomed to inhale.

Frequent and loud complaints are uttered, both by transient and stationary residents, against the filthy streets, villanous smells, licensed swine and other nuisances, equally hard to endure, which are so peculiarly the characteristics of Pittsburgh. The police is so wretchedly organized, and so remiss in the performance of its duties, that, unless it be in the dry time of mid-summer, a lady's slipper cannot be worn after more than one promenade in the streets, with any moderate deference to neatness and fashion. Even the more mire-defying, water-proof boots of the gentlemen run great risk of having their polish so much sullied, by an attempt to cross one of the avenues, as to be utterly unfit for public exhibition, before they have received another varnishing. A solitary lamp twinkles here and there, over the door of a tavern, or on the sign post, whenever the moon is in its first or last quarter. The rest of the city is involved in primeval darkness; and he who is adventurous enough to tread the narrow space between the front of the houses and the curb-stone, after the departure of the sun, must use special caution to avoid a trip into the gutter, or a tumble over some box, barrel, or other obstacle, which may chance to be placed in his path. Not far remote, some attempts were made to enlighten our principal streets, by placing lamps near some nut-shell watchboxes, which were erected at intervals "few and far between." This improvement being found too expensive, the watch-boxes were abandoned, and the few lamps that had escaped the ravages of mischievous boys, were taken down. With all these crying and trying perils, inconveniences and wants, which daily and nightly beset them, the great majority of our citizens are doggedly contented with their place of abode. They stoutly maintain, that, when the projected water-works, the national armory, and the grand canals shall be completed; when the obstructions in the Ohio, above Wheeling are removed, and when the contemplated indications of immense improvement, in and about the city, are realized, we shall be the most manufacturing, commercial, and altogether flourishing community west of the mountains, not excepting *Wheeling*, Cincinnati, or Louisville.

The population of our melancholy city, has within a few years, increased, beyond the greatest ratio, that is usually adopted in calculations relative to human accumulation. Composed, (with our own countrymen,) of almost all European nations, tongues and languages, it might be supposed to exhibit many varieties of character. But the similarity of occupations and intentions, which generally prevails in towns almost exclusively manufacturing, has given to the disposition and habitudes of our citizens, that predominating cast, which is so obvious to all attentive observers; and which is varied only by the slight shades, that always, and every where, distinguish human society. The great pervading trait in their character, is derived from a rigid observance of many thrifty rules prescribed by " Poor Richard," in his economical and practical lectures. They are a bustling, pains-taking, money-making people; always ready to increase the stock of their worldly goods, by an adherence to the maxim of wise political economists, "buy cheap and sell dear." Not that, by any manner of means, they practice any impositions on the necessity or credulity of their customers. They " keep on hand, and have constantly for sale," articles of the very best quality; and use no other arts besides their own peculiar, in disposing of their wares, than those which the most conscientious christians employ, while they watch the market, and take all allowable advantages of the " balance of trade." In the polite circles, there is a laudable deference observed for the ancient and judicious rules laid down in the code of *fashion*. We have our casts of society, graduated and divided with as much regard to rank and dignity as the most scrupulous Hindoos maintain, in the defence of their religious prejudices. Wealth is held in high honour, and is a most potent agent in bringing down the hills, and filling up the vallies of etiquette. Between the several classes, of which our society is composed, there are lines of demarcation drawn, wide, distinct, and not to be violated with impunity. There are few who boast their noble lineage, display any heraldric emblazoning, or nourish genealogical trees, deep-rooted, and sending forth wide-spreading branches. To supply these deficiencies, they unrol their own deeds, or those of their ancestors, (not in *arms*, but) containing their *titles*—to boundless tracts of land in the country adjacent, or to lots in the town, with the appurtenances. They speak modestly, of their stock in bank, and stock in trade; for it is considered no derogation from family consequence, to be concerned in trade, in this palpably trading community.

The days of simple happiness, which were once enjoyed upon the banks of our two, aye, three pleasant streams, are gone, and it would be very silly to mourn over them. Still, we cannot help looking back, with sorrowful heart, on that time of unaffected content and gaiety, when the unambitious people who were domiciled in the village of " Fort Pitt," or the yet unchartered town of Pittsburgh, were ignorant and careless of all the invidious distinctions, which distract and divide the inhabitants of overgrown cities. Then, all was peaceful heart-felt felicity, undisturbed by the rankling thorns of envy; and equality, without the intervention of demagogues, was the tie which united all ranks and conditions in one community. The social virtues were the household gods, whom men revered, as the beneficent protectors of character and property, which no one dared to invade, because they were the common possession of all. The long winter evenings were passed by the humble villagers, at each others homes, with merry tale and song, or in simple games; and the hours of night sped lightly onward, with the unskilled, untiring youth, as they threaded the mazes of the dance, guided by the music of the violin, from which some good humoured rustic drew his Orphean sounds. In the jovial time of harvest and haymaking, the sprightly and active of the village, participated in the rural labours and the hearty pastimes, which distinguish that happy season. The balls and merry makings, that were so frequent in the village, were attended by all, without any particular deference to rank or riches.

No other etiquette, than that which natural politeness prescribed, was exacted or expected. Social intercourse was
unrestrained by the cold, formal, insipid ceremonies, that
deprive it of more than half its attractions. Young fellows
might pay their devoirs to their female acquaintance; ride,
walk or talk with them, and pass hours in their society,
without being looked upon with suspicion by parents, or
slandered by trolloping gossips. Old bachelors were then
much less numerous than they have become, since the lowly
village has been metamorphosed into a city, & the belles are
so anxious, on the third visit at farthest, to discover the real
intentions of their gallants, that they deter them from a
fourth call, by their "side-long looks" and indirect inqui-
ries, as to the object which they have in view; and by an ex-
cess of prudery and policy, confirm them in their resolu-
tions of celibacy, if they had ever formed any; for now

> "Talk six times with the same single lady,
> And you may get the wedding dresses ready."

This tedious account of village employments, recrea-
tions, and single ladies and gentlemen, who had as little
objection to be married, as any city beau or belle can have,
may furnish a description of the manners and customs of
many a little town, as well as of that which Pittsburgh, now
a mighty city, once was. Yet, what have we gained by
our growth in wealth and population, in manufactures,
trade, and all other desirable things, compared with the
artless manners, and delightful amusements, which we have
lost? Chartered as we are, by act of assembly, as a city
corporation, do we enjoy the real, unfashionable contentment with which our village predecessors were blessed?
Where are our pleasant, social tea-drinkings; our sturdy
blind-man's buff; our evening chit-chat, in which both
sexes participated, without a thought of visiting cards,
morning calls or preconcerted "accidentals?" Where are
the strawberry huntings; the unclassed balls; the charming
promenades, of which all partook with light hearts, and
careless of fashionable ceremonies? Now, we have no places even of *fashionable* resort, or rather, places which polite and fashionable people frequent; where pleasure might
be sought and found, or where the useful could be mingled
with the agreeable. Many of us are, as a direct consequence, often sadly at a loss how to dispose of a leisure
hour, which, by the bye, seldom breaks in upon the en-
gagements of any other class of our population, than that

of the lawyers, who are said to sleep out the vacations; or the physicians, who are sometimes, during unfortunate seasons of general health, compelled to lay aside their lancets, "for lack of argument." There would be an utter deficiency of classical shades and temples of literature and science, were it not for the nominal existence of the "Western University of Pennsylvania," founded and endowed by an act of our state legislature; the "Buildings" of which, whilom occupied as an "Academy," are situated on the corner of Third street and Cherry alley. It possesses a very respectable faculty, the greatest proportion of whom, however, seldom fill their respective chairs. In addition to this distinguished seat of learning, there are numerous private seminaries, where reading, writing, and other ordinary branches of education are flourishing; a few debating clubs, and the neucleus of a law society, which we beg pardon for omitting in a former paragraph. The novels of the "Great unknown" and Cooper, are read by all the reading ladies and gentlemen, whenever they can be obtained. But as we have no other circulating library, than that which is styled the "Apprentices," and the booksellers do not cater very liberally for the lovers of light reading, the latest and best works in this department of literature, that come to us, are few in number, and have to accommodate so many borrowers, that they grow old, long before their admirers can be favoured with a perusal of them. No public reading room is open, for the reception of those who might prefer a literary lounge, or rational enjoyment, to the orgies of the gaming table, and the social, though more sensual pleasures of the tavern. More than one desperate attempt has been made to establish and continue such a praise worthy institution; but every such struggle was unblessed and unavailing, probably because our boetian atmosphere is adverse to all intellectual improvement, and fatal to literary taste, or because the more substantial and lucrative avocations of trade, which are prosecuted with so much enthusiasm by our citizens, have deprived them of all inclination for pursuits merely mental. To make amends for such unsuccessful adventures, we have several newspapers, each of which may be enjoyed by the quidnuncs, at least once a week; and one or two of them may be considered as "large and respectable." As we have not much genius of domestic growth to boast, no valuable publications issue from the letter-press of our metropolis, with

the exception of almanacs, containing wise prognostics con-
cerning the weather; *very interesting* tracts; the Ohio and
Mississippi Navigator; neatly covered primers, and spel-
ling books, equal to those of *Noah Webster* himself.   No
public garden within the city, or its environs, affords a
retreat from the drudgery of business, the heat of the sun,
or the smoke of the chimnies.   The only temple dedicated
to histrionic representations, of which we might, but will
not boast, is the diminutive, wretched and woe-begone
edifice in Third street, now rarely occupied, except by
occasional itinerant sleight-of-hand professors, and rope
dancers.   Its dilapidated condition, resulting from the
united ravages of time, and of those doers of all mischief,
the boys, has rendered it entirely unsuitable for the
residence of Thalia and Melpemone.   Other genteel
rational amusements, besides such as the theatre might
afford, are equally difficult of attainment.   Sunday is a
fearfully long and wearisome day for the most of us.   They
who do not choose to attend one of our numerous churches;
who cannot afford to take a canter on horseback, or pay
for a seat in a hack, as far as the Arsenal, Gillespie's, or
Noodle Doosey, in the pleasant time of the year, must be
content to promenade the streets; saunter to the bank of
the Monongahela to view the steam boats; stroll across one
of the bridges, or climb the hills that, look down so in-
vitingly upon us.

Population and Buildings.

According to the census taken this year, by Mr. Joseph Barclay, it
appears that the City contains the following population : —

Males under 20 years,	2663	Excess of males, 206
Females under 18,	2457	
Males over 20 and under 40,	1740	Excess of males, 5
Females over 18 and under 35,	1735	
Males over 40 and under 60,	557	Excess of males, 45
Females over 35 and under 50,	532	
Males over 60,	111	Excess of females, 165
Females over 50,	276	
Coloured people,	424	

Total, 10,515   Ex. of males in all 91.
Of these 2303 were born in a foreign country.
The population of Pittsburgh in 1820, was 7248, presenting in the
year 1826, an increase of 3267.

The population of the suburbs of Pittsburgh, as taken during the present month, is as follows :—

KENSINGTON.

Males under 20 years,	107	Excess of males,	41
Females under 18,	66		
Males over 20 and under 40,	50	Excess of females,	2
Females over 18 and under 35,	52		
Males over 40 and under 60,	30	Excess of males,	17
Females over 35 and under 50,	13		
Males over 60,	4	Excess of females,	8
Females over 50,	7		

Total, 329 Total ex. of females, 53

Of these 120 are of foreign birth.

BIRMINGHAM.

Males under 20,	133	Excess of males,	5
Females under 18,	128		
Males over 20 and under 40,	64	Excess of males,	3
Females over 18 and under 35,	61		
Males over 40 and under 60,	28	Excess of males,	1
Females over 35 and under 50,	27		
Males over 60,	5	Excess of females,	8
Females over 50,	13		

Total, 459 Total ex. of males, 1

Of these 117 are foreigners.

NORTHERN LIBERTIES.

Males under 20 years,	197	Excess of females,	14
Females under 18,	211		
Males over 20 and not above 40,	104	Excess of females,	3
Females over 18 and not over 35,	107		
Males over 40 and not above 60,	42	Excess of males,	14
Females over 35 and not above 50,	28		
Males over 60,	5	Excess of females,	12
Females over 50,	17		

Total, 711 Total ex. of females, 15

Of these 228 are of foreign birth.

ALLEGHENY TOWN.

Males under 20 years,	214		
Females under 18,	214		
Males over 20 and not over 40,	88	Excess of females,	15
Females over 18 and not above 35,	103		
Males over 40 and under 60,	34	Excess of males,	1
Females over 35 and under 50,	33		
Males over 60,	4	Excess of females,	8
Females over 50,	12		

Total, 702 Total ex. of females, 22

Of these 75 were born in a foreign country.

RECAPITULATION.

Pittsburgh,	10,515
Kensington,	329
Birmingham,	459
Northern Liberties,	711
Allegheny Town,	702
Miscellaneous population residing in the suburbs,	260
Grand total,	12,976
Total excess of females,	108
Whole number of foreigners	2863

From an examination made a few weeks since, the City presents within its boundaries 1873 buildings, composing 2360 tenements, and are as follows.—

Of brick,	3 stories high,			155
Of do.	2 do.	do.		340
Of stone,	2 do.	do.		10
Of frame,	3 do.	do.		10
Of do.	2 do.	do.		623
Of do.	1 do.	do.		280
Churches and public buildings, all brick,				17
Shops, Factories, Mills, &c. &c.				438
			Total,	1873

Of these, there are occupied as

Dwellings,	1140
Places of worship, and other public buildings,	17
Stores,	51
Groceries,	136
Banks,	2
Taverns,	16
Factories, Mills, Shops, &c.	438
Warehouses and other buildings,	73
	1873

There will be put up this year, a great number of brick and frame buildings—of brick, some very handsome blocks will be erected.

In Kensington, there are 40 buildings, composing about 60 tenements—all frame but 4, which are of brick.

In Birmingham, there are 65 buildings, forming about 90 tenements, of which 16 are brick and the balance generally, two story frames.

The Northern Liberties gives 84 buildings, composing 127 tenements, of which 27 are brick, and the remainder two story frame buildings, factories, &c.

In Allegheny Town there are 85 houses, forming about 93 tenements—of which 13 are brick, and the balance, good two story frames, generally.

TOTALS.

Number of buildings in Pittsburgh and suburbs,	2147
Number of tenements which they compose,	2525

MANUFACTURES.

NO town in the United States, at an equal distance from the ocean, enjoys so many advantages tending to manufacturing prosperity, as are possessed by Pittsburgh. Placed at the head of the Ohio, which yields in magnitude and beauty to few streams in the world, it is the store house, as well of the mechanic arts, as of great commercial wealth, and is the seat of a population that supplies a vast extent of the western regions with the products of ingenuity and industry. The facilities of communication which are opened for it, with this range of country, through the Ohio and Mississippi, and their tributaries, secure to it a superiority over almost every other town in the Union. Its resources, furnished by nature, for the prosecution of all the mechanical pursuits, are inexhaustible.

The year 1810, may be said to have been the commencement of Pittsburgh manufactures. Then a few enterprizing men began the fabrication of cottons ,woollens, glass, &c. and from this time until the year 1815, its prosperity and increase was unrivalled—so great indeed, and sudden was its rise from an obscure and retired borough, to rank and importance, that it became the theme of much notoriety, as well in our own country as in Europe. In England, Pittsburgh was called the Birmingham of America. The war however, which existed about this period, between the United States and Great Britain, was the great promoter of our prosperity; for as long as foreign commerce was depressed, so long our manufactures succeeded. Landed property commanded an immense price—all kinds of labour as well as the produce of it, had an unusual value set upon it—in fact, such was the rage to acquire fortunes, by taking advantage of circumstances, that a complete speculating mania reigned throughout the country. The private citizen drew forth his earnings of former days to vest it in manufactures; the merchant dived deep into the business of his calling, and the farmer who lived comfortably upon his paternal estate with all the necessary comforts of life

5

about him, took to land jobbing speculations, with an uncommon avidity. But the peace, alas! put an end to all these visions of wealth, and harvests of prosperity. The channels of commerce were immediately opened, and the vast quantities of British goods, that, unsold, had lain in the ware-houses of the English manufacturers for two years before, now inundated the country, and were thrown into market at any price. American fabrics immediately depreciated. The merchant who had made his purchases previously, at high prices, failed; the manufactories slowly declined, until at last many of them stood still—and the speculator lost all that he had bought, and was probably, compelled to sell the little he had when he commenced his schemes of aggrandizement. The distresses that followed this event, can only be known by those who were concerned in them, or witnessed their dire effects; and it is only within a year or two, that the people are beginning to recover from the difficulties of that at once fortunate and unfortunate period. We trust, however, as we have heretofore observed, that the prosperity of Pittsburgh, which is now reviving under such bright and happy auspices, is founded on a permanent basis, free from those chimeras and doubtful chances, which from the effects of national conflicts, or human ambition, like bubbles, rise, swell and expand.

IRON.

THE fabrication of iron, being one of the most important branches of our manufactures, and being one of the great staple commodities of the country, we shall first notice those establishments, in and about Pittsburgh, where it is made.

SLIGO ROLLING MILL.

This establishment is situated on the south side of the Monongahela river, immediately opposite the mouth of Market Street, and is owned by Messrs. ROBERT T. STEWART and JOHN LYON. It was erected in 1825, but during the winter of that year, was partly consumed, by its accidentally taking fire. However, in a few weeks, it was again put in operation. Sligo mill may be considered as a branch of those extensive iron-works which the proprietors own on the Juniata, as all the iron they make use of, is brought from there in a state partly manufactured, that is, in large blocks, called blooms, which do not require the process of puddling, but are immediately fit for rolling. The consumption of blooms at the Sligo mill, is about 900 tons annually. The engine is one of the most powerful in or about Pittsburgh, being 130 horse, and was built by Mark Stackhouse; some idea may be formed of the strength and immensity of the various machinery, when we say that their weight is 120 tons. Thirty hands are employed daily in the different departments, and the consumption of coal per annum is about 90,000 bushels. The value of bar, boiler, nail and sheet iron, &c. manufactured per year, is 99,000 dollars.

We have spoken to several mechanical gentlemen who were competent to judge, of the qualities of our Pittsburgh iron, and they stated, unequivocally, that the iron made at Sligo mill was not surpassed by any in the U. States.

A short time since an order was sent to Mr. Stewart from the National works at Harper's Ferry, for a load of Sligo iron, to be converted into musket barrels, as an experiment upon its qualities—we have not yet heard the result, but should it succeed, the advantages that might accrue to this concern would be of considerable importance.

JUNIATA IRON WORKS.

Situated on the Allegheny river, in the Northern Liberties; is owned by Dr. Peter Shoenberger. They were erected in 1824, and may also be considered as a distant branch of the extensive forges of the proprietor on the waters of the Juniata. The establishment here is a very extensive one, embracing a large lot of land, with large and convenient frame and brick buildings. The machinery of the works is of the very best and most substantial kind, and in its location, presents great economy and regularity. The whole was put up under the superintendance of M. B. Belknap, Esq. who, as an engineer and ingenious mechanic, has few equals in the western country. The engine is of 120 horse power, and was built by Mr. Mathew Smith, now of the firm of Binny and Smith. The weight of castings composing the machinery is 95 tons.

There is annually converted into bar, boiler, nail and sheet-iron, rods, &c. 500 tons of pig metal and 500 tons of blooms, principally brought from the Juniata. The yearly consumption of coal is 129.700 bushels, and the value of iron manufactured during the last 12 months, was 88,000 dollars.

Of Dr. Shoenberger's iron, we can only say that its reputation as being of superior quality, has long since been established. The competent knowledge which Dr. S. possesses as it regards the fabrication of iron, and the assiduous personal attention which he continually pays to the various departments of his concern, will always sustain the good fame of "*Shoenberger's Iron.*"

GRANT'S HILL IRON WORKS,

Owned by Messrs. WILLIAM H. HAYS and DAVID ADAMS, was erected in 1821. The machinery is put in operation by a steam engine of eighty horse power, built by the Columbian Steam Engine Company. Thirty hands are daily employed. There has been manufactured within the last year, into bar, boiler, nail and hoop iron, rods, &c. 600 tons of pig metal, and 200 tons of blooms. The yearly consumption of coal is 90,000 bushels, and the total value of iron made, during the past year, was 67,000 dollars.

UNION ROLLING MILL,

Situated on the eastern boundary of the city, in Kensington, and owned by Messrs. BALDWIN, ROBINSON, M'NICKLE AND BELTZHOOVER. This is the largest and most extensive establishment of the kind in the western country. The machinery is driven by two steam engines of 100 horse power each, which were built by the Columbian Steam Engine Company in the year 1819, and the weight of castings and wrought iron required in their construction is immense, being 500,000 pounds. The quantity of metal coverted last year into bar, sheet and boiler iron, &c. was about 1500 tons, which upon an average is worth 100 dollars per ton, making the total value of their manufacture about 150,000 dollars. Attached to the mill, is an extensive nail factory, where 6½ tons of iron, are weekly converted into nails of all sizes. Of this, however, we shall speak in another place. The whole number of hands employed is 100, and the consumption of coal per annum, 182000 bushels.

DOWLAIS IRON WORKS,

In Kensington, erected in 1825, by Mr. Lewis. Has an engine of 100 horse power, and manufactures bar iron from the pig. This establishment is not now in operation, owing to some unforeseen difficulties—but we understand that preparations are making to continue it as vigorously as ever. It is capable of making about 600 tons of iron per year.

PITTSBURGH ROLLING MILL,

Corner of Penn Street and Cecil's alley, established in 1812, by C. Cowan, now owned by R. Bowen. Has an engine of 70 horse power, built by the Columbian Steam Engine Company, which drives one pair of rolls and slitters and 10 nail machines. In this mill there is no other than *bar* iron made use of, of which 500 tons is annually made into boiler, sheet and nail iron, and rods for nails and spikes. There are 21 hands constantly employed, and 30000 bushels of coal consumed per annum. The value of the various kinds of rolled iron made per year, is about 70,000 dollars.

PINE CREEK ROLLING MILL, &c.

Owned by M. B. Belknap, Esq. situate on Pine creek, a few miles above Pittsburgh. Has an engine of 100 horse power, which is employed in rolling bar iron into boiler, sheet, and nail iron, rods, &c. At this establishment, both steam and water power are employed, and the manufacture of axes, scythes, sickles, shovels, &c. is carried on to great extent: about 40 hands are employed, and about 600 tons of bar iron made use of annually. Mr. Belknap contemplates making iron from the pig, in a short time.

RECAPITULATION.

		hands.	tons.	value.	coal consumed.
Union Rolling Mill,		100	1500	150000	182000
Pittsburgh	do.	21	500	70000	30000
Sligo	do.	30	900	99000	90000
Juniata	do.	60	800	88000	129700
Grant's Hill	do.	30	900	67000	90000
Pine creek	do.	40	600	85000	40000
		181	4900	559,000	601,700

5

AIR FOUNDERIES.

THERE are few even in our city, who are aware of the immense business that has been done, and is now doing in these establishments. There are no less than eight of them in full operation.

THE PITTSBURGH FOUNDRY,

Was erected as early as the year 1804, by Mr. Joseph M'Clurg, and was the first establishment of the kind west of the mountains. The opposition that Mr. M. met with from his friends shows how limited the views of the citizens of that period were, in relation to the important situation of Pittsburgh, and the great sources of wealth that lay around it. Many thought at that time, that Mr. M'Clurg would certainly be ruined—that a foundry was useless—and that he could not possibly succeed—he persevered however, and subsequent years have shown the fallacy of human prognostications—he realized a fortune—has retired from business, and left the old foundry to fill the pockets of his successors with better stuff than pig metal.

During the last war Mr. M'Clurg had a very large contract with the national government, for furnishing ordnance and ball. The principal part of which were destined for the fleet on Lake Erie. The Arsenal at Lawrenceville exhibits a long range of field pieces, carronades, &c. of his manufacture, that are as beautiful as they are substantial and true—they having stood all those nice and scrupulous tests of strength and measurement, which the ordnance department are wont to use in their inspections.

The Pittsburgh foundry is at present carried on by Messrs. ALEXANDER M'CLURG, CUTHBERT and CUDDY, on an extensive scale. There are two furnaces which are daily in use and the amount of metal that is converted into wheels, shafts, cannon, stoves, hollow ware, grates and all manner of castings, is about 600 tons per annum. From 25 to 30 hands are constantly employed and yearly about 15000 bushels of coal are consumed. The value of castings is from 65 to 70 dollars per ton, consequently the manufactures of this foundry amount to 40,800 dollars per annum. Of the castings made during the past year, about 300 tons found a market in Ohio, Kentucky, Indiana, &c.

The present proprietors have now a large contract with

government for furnishing 90 pieces of ordnance, from 6
to 24 pounders. To gentlemen who are fond of particular-
ities or who are ignorant of the scrupulous exactness with
which the business of the ordnance department is conducted at Washington, it would be worth a walk to the foundry,
to see the drawing of a 24 pounder. Beside the master
hand that is visible in the sketch, there is nothing can surpass the correctness with which every part is laid down,
and the minuteness with which every "jot and tittle" is
required to be executed.

In order to facilitate the operations of boring these pieces, the contractors intend to put up this summer, a steam
boring mill, to which will be attached machinery for
turning, grinding, &c. This branch being heretofore done
by horse power.

M'Clurg & Co have two large ware-houses—one at the
foundry, corner of Smithfield and Fifth streets, and the
other in Wood, between Front and Water streets, where
may be seen some fine specimens and patterns in their line.

JACKSON FOUNDRY,

Corner of Sixth and Liberty streets—owned by Messrs.
KINGSLAND, LIGHTNER and SOWERS, and erected in 1823.
At this establishment during the past year, there has been
made, some of the heaviest castings ever seen in this country. About 300 tons of pig metal are converted here annually into machinery of all kinds; stoves, grates, wagon
boxes, plough plates, and in short, every article that may
be desired, from the weight of 4 tons down to ¼ of a pound.
Twenty hands are generally employed, and about 9000
bushels of coal consumed yearly.

EAGLE FOUNDRY,

In Kensington. This establishment was erected by A.
BEELEN, but is now conducted by the same gentlemen that
own the Jackson foundry, and composes a part of their
concern. The castings of both foundries are much the
same. The consumption of metal at the Eagle is about
250 tons yearly. Employs about 12 hands, and burns a-
bout 7000 bushels of coal. The value of castings of both
establishments amount annually to about 86.750 dollars.
As to the various articles manufactured at these foundries,
it would not be hazarding our veracity by saying they
were of the first order. The gentlemen who conduct the

mechanical operations, are two of our ablest moulders, whose capabilities and knowledge of their avocation are above being questioned. And as they combine every attention and skill, with their own actual and unremitted labour, the reputation of the Jackson and Eagle foundries, will always be maintained, while they are concerned. We allude to Messrs. Kingsland and Sowers.

Their warehouse is on Liberty near Sixth street, where are every variety of castings and patterns.

PHŒNIX FOUNDRY,

Situate on Scotch hill, corner of Ross and Third streets; owned by Messrs. MILLER and FREEMAN. It was established in 1821, by —— Clark, and is principally devoted to the lighter order of castings—such as sad-irons, grates, stoves, wheels, &c. &c. into which about 200 tons are annually converted. Ten hands are constantly employed, and about 7800 bushels of coal are consumed annually.— The value of castings made during the last year, amounts to 14560 dollars.

This concern we believe is in a very prosperous condition, and as it is owned by a couple of industrious, clever gentlemen, we wish it may continue so. They have a ware-house in Liberty, three doors south of St. Clair street.

STACKHOUSE'S FOUNDRY,

Attached to the Columbian Steam Engine factory, in Front street, at the corner of Redoubt alley. The principal part of the castings made at this establishment, are steam machinery, into which about 300 tons of metal are annually converted. Constant employment is given to 12 hands, and about 7800 bushels are consumed yearly. The value of the manufactures per year, is about 18000 dollars.

ALLEGHENY FOUNDRY,

Situated near the Allegheny river, on M'Cormick's alley, and owned by Mr. WILLIAM FRANKLIN; was erected in 1822. Manufactures light articles generally, consuming per annum, about 156 tons of metal, and employs 6 hands. The consumption of coal is about 4000 bushels, and the value of manufactures during the last year 10,140 dollars.

STACKHOUSE AND THOMPSON'S FOUNDRY,

On Liberty and Second streets ; erected in 1824, and is attached to their steam engine factory. The whole of the castings made here are applied to steam boats and steam machinery, generally. The quantity of metal made use of last year, was about 120 tons, employs from 5 to 7 hands, and annually consumes about 3500 bushels of coal. The value of machinery made in the same time, is about $7200.

PRICE'S CUPOLA FURNACE,

Situated one fourth of a mile east of Pittsburgh, and may be considered a brass as well as an iron foundry, as all the various articles of a light nature in both branches are manufactured here. Mr. Price also makes large crucibles for fusing copper, brass, &c. and is the only person about Pittsburgh, who has succeeded in making these articles in perfection. Value of castings, &c. about 4000 dollars.

BIRMINGHAM FOUNDRY,

Carried on by Messrs. SUTTON and NICHOLSON, consumes annually about 200 tons of metal, which is converted into castings of every kind, and valued at 12000 dollars. This foundry is connected with other establishments, which we shall notice in another place. Consumption of coal about 10000 bushels, and employs eight hands.

There is also manufactured at this establishment, by steam machinery, tobacco-press, paper-mill and fuller's screws of all sizes. Iron turning of all kinds, is also done.

RECAPITULATION.

In the eight foundries before mentioned, there has been converted into castings, during the last twelve months, 2126 tons of metal, 106 hands employed—65,000 bushels of coal consumed, and the total value of manufactures, 132,610 dollars.

••••●●●••••

NAILERIES.

THE manufacture of nails is carried on here to a very great extent; so much so, that it is probable there are more nails made in Pittsburgh in one year than is made in the same period in all the western country beside. The invention of those patent nail machines have produced a great revolution in this branch of business, and have almost entirely superseded the use of the hammer and the die. Our readers may form an idea of the facility with which the cutting and heading of nails is performed when we state that of 3d nails 400 may be made per minute; of 6d 300 to 350, and of 12d there has been made 1760 pounds per day, on one machine.

UNION ROLLING MILL NAIL FACTORY,

Has 14 nail machines in operation, by which all kinds of nails are manufactured, from 3d to 20d. There was made last year at this establishment, 720,000 lbs. which being averaged at 6 cents per pound, gives their value at 43200 dollars.

SLIGO NAIL FACTORY,

Attached to the Sligo Rolling Mill, and driven by steam; has 4 machines, that cut annually, 400000 pounds of nails, which are worth 32,000 dollars.

PITTSBURGH NAIL FACTORY,

Owned by Richard Bowen, and connected with his Rolling Mill, has 10 machines. During the present year, there was manufactured at this concern, 5804 kegs of cut nails, of various sizes, and 22000 pounds of wrought nails; making a total of 782,887 pounds. Value $66,544 39 cts.

GRANT'S HILL NAIL FACTORY,

Attached to the Grant's Hill Iron works, has five machines, which are driven by steam; manufactures 250 tons of nails, of various sizes, per annum. Value, 40,000 dollars.

JUNIATA NAIL FACTORY,

Connected with the Juniata iron works, and owned by Dr. Shoenberger. Has 5 machines in operation, and manufactures per annum, 500000 pounds of nails, of all sizes.— Value, 40,000 dollars.

PINE CREEK NAIL FACTORY,

Owned by Mr. B. Belknap, Esq. and connected with his other extensive works on that stream. There was made at this establishment last year, by 4 machines, about 3640 kegs of nails, of various sizes, making 456000 pounds.— Valued at 34,100 dollars.

There are in Pittsburgh, about 6 factories, where nails are made in the old way; employ about 16 hands, and make per annum, 360000 pounds. Valued at 28000 dollars.

RECAPITULATION.

	weight.	value.
Union Rolling Mill Factory,	720,000	$ 43200
Sligo do. do. do.	400,000	32000
Pittsburgh do. do.	782,887	86544
Grant's Hill do. do.	500,000	30000
Juniata do. do.	500,000	40000
Pine creek do.	457,000	34100
Miscellaneous factories,	360,000	28800
Total,	3,708,887	$273644

STEAM ENGINES.

PITTSBURGH, in this branch of business, has acquired great celebrity. The numerous engines which have been made here, and the attention that has been paid to their construction, has enabled our engineers, beyond all others, to improve upon them, by rendering every succeeding one less complicated, simplifying its movements and rendering its operations less difficult and dangerous. It may be said, without an exception, that there is no place in the world, that can surpass Pittsburgh, as to the means and materials, which it affords for the manufacture of these powerful machines. The talent and knowledge, too, of applying the power, and compelling it to act in the various ways required, are possessed by our mechanics in all necessary perfection.

The generality of Pittsburgh engines, are constructed on what is called the high pressure principle, in contra-distinction to the *low* pressure. Of the merits of either we are not competent to decide, each has a powerful support in the prejudices of the people; but were we to judge from the great majority of high pressure engines in use, and the generally superior running of boats that are propelled by them, we would give the preference unequivocally to high steam. As to danger, which a great many persons suppose is always connected with high steam, we can say from an account that has been kept of accidents which have occured on the Ohio, and elsewhere, that the number on board the low pressure steam boats, have been twice, if not three times as great as those on high pressure ones.

There are six steam engine manufactories in Pittsburgh and its vicinity, all actively engaged, where engines can be furnished 15 per cent. lower than at any other establishments of the kind in the United States.

COLUMBIAN STEAM ENGINE COMPANY,

At the corner of Second street and Redoubt alley, conducted by Mr. MARK STACKHOUSE, a gentleman of known reputation as an able engineer, and who in company with Messrs. Rogers, Evans and others, were the first persons that commenced this branch of business in the western country. During the past year, there has been made at this establishment, *seven* steam engines, none of which were less than 60 horse power, and their average value was, 30,000 dollars. In their construction and for other purposes, they made use of 100,000 lbs. of bar iron, besides the necessary quantity of castings. 20 hands are constantly employed, and about 4500 bushels of coal consumed. A very large high pressure engine is now finishing for a steam boat on Lake Erie.

Connected with the Columbian Steam Engine Factory, there is a turning, boring and grinding establishment, which is put into operation by steam power, derived from the Pittsburgh Steam Mill. Here are cut all kinds of tobacco-press, paper-makers and fullers screws; turning of iron, &c.

A better evidence of the high estimation in which our steam engines are held, could not be given, than by quoting the fact, that a few months since, Mr. Stackhouse received an order for an engine of 100 horse power, to be placed in the iron works of the Messrs. Thompsons, at the mouth of French creek, on the Schuylkill, 25 miles from Philadelphia. It was built, accordingly, and forwarded over the mountains in wagons, and has fully realized every expectation, as to its excellence.

Messrs. WARDEN AND ARTHURS,

At the corner of Second and West streets, have an extensive concern. These gentlemen have been very successful in their various engines they have made, and their work is held in deservedly high estimation. During the last year they put up *five* engines, all of the larger class, valued at 35000 dollars. They employ about 30 hands, and consume 5000 bushels of coal per year. A large and powerful low pressure engine is now finishing at this establishment, for a steam boat on Lake Erie.

For the purpose of facilitating the operations of turning, punching, &c. and reducing the quantity of manual labour required, the proprietors intend putting up a steam engine this year.

Messrs. STACKHOUSE AND THOMPSON,

On Liberty street at the corner of Third. This firm has put up some of the best engines employed in the navigation of the western waters. They have constructed within the last year, 5 engines of the largest class, valued at 35000 dollars. Thirty hands are daily employed.

Messrs. SMITH AND BINNY,

On Grant's Hill. These gentlemen have lately commenced, but they have already built 3 engines, valued at 14000 dollars, and employ 15 hands.

M. B. BELKNAP, Esq.

On Pine creek; has made within the last year, two very large engines, and has two others on hand, valued at 16000 dollars.

MAHLON ROGERS,

at the corner of Grant and Fourth streets. Has made two small engines, valued at 800. Two large ones are now on hand.

RECAPITULATION.

Columbian Steam Engine Company,	7	30000
Warden and Arthurs,	5	35000
Stackhouse and Thompson,	5	35000
Smith and Binny,	3	14000
M. B. Belknap,	2	8000
M. Rogers,	2	800
	24	122,800
On hand,	6 worth	30,000
Total,	30	$ 152,800

105 hands employed in all.

6

At the different factories, several engines are contracted for, to be put up this summer and fall, and it is highly probable their number this year will exceed that of the last.

STEAM WIRE FACTORY,

In Kensington, near the Union Rolling Mill, conducted by Mr. ARNOLD EICHBAUM. This establishment was put up in 1810, and was carried on a few years, very successfully; but on the conclusion of the late war, the depression of prices compelled the proprietor to shut up. It was re-established last year—has an engine of 10 horse power—employs seven hands, and manufactures wire from No. 1 to 16. We have been informed by gentlemen who are acquainted with the article, that Mr. Eichbaum's wire is of an excellent quality.

STEAM TURNING AND GRINDING MILL,

Owned by Mr. WILLIAM HALL, in Kensington. This is a very useful concern. It is devoted entirely to turning brass and iron, and to grinding sad irons, &c. &c. Has an engine of 10 horse power.

In conclusion of our notice of the iron business, and the various branches connected with it, we think it not amiss to state that beside the vast quantities of Juniata bar iron that is constantly transported from that stream, there were brought to Pittsburgh within the last 12 months about 5000 tons of pig metal. This immense amount was supplied from about 12 or 13 blast furnaces, situated in the neighbouring counties of Beaver, Butler, Fayette, Westmoreland, Venango, Crawford, &c.

COTTON.

THE manufactures of Cotton, which in the eastern states and in Europe, employ so large a proportion of wealth, skill and industry, have, as yet, been established here, but to a limited extent. The large amount of capital, the various tributary and connected branches of workmanship, indispensably necessary to profitable operation, have probably prevented its earlier and more successful experiment. Enough, however, has been done, to exhibit the.

advantages arising to the community, and we have no doubt, if we were possessed of the overflowing wealth and population of the districts already mentioned, the requisite mechanical ingenuity and skill could be supplied, and that we should no longer suffer our western brethren to supply themselves from abroad.

The first experiment worthy of notice, instituted here, was that of Hugh and James Jelly, during the late war. Their establishment, however, was prostrated in its infancy, by the deluge of foreign goods which peace poured in upon our unconfirmed and struggling institutions, not as yet supported by a protecting tariff, nor even cherished by public sentiment or national partiality. So disastrous was their example, that, for years, none durst risk the fate of these unfortunate pioneers, and their factory stood at the entrance of Pittsburgh, deserted and decayed, a melancholy presage to the stranger who visited us, of the general gloom and dulness which pervaded the city.

In was not until the year 1819 that a new essay in the cotton business was made.

JAMES ARTHURS & SONS' STEAM COTTON FACTORY,

Situated on Strawberry, near Cherry alley. The machinery consists of one throstle of 120 spindles, one mule of 168 spindles, with the necessary apparatus for carding, &c. It is principally employed in the manufacture of fine yarns from No. 16 to 20. Thirteen hands are employed in the cotton factory. In a Woollen Factory, owned by the same firm, adjoining the above, and propelled by the same steam engine, a very large amount of country business is done, and some looms are employed in the manufacture of cassinets. Of this further notice may be taken under another head.

PHŒNIX STEAM COTTON FACTORY,

Owned by Messrs. JAMES ADAMS, ALLEN & GRANT and JAMES S. CRAFT—is erected on the ruins of that of the Messrs. Jellys, in the Northern Liberties of the city. It was reserved for these gentlemen to introduce among us, all the improved skill, and valuable inventions, which our Yankee brethren have ingrafted upon European importations. In the spring of 1822, they brought from Providence, (R. I.) the largest amount of machinery ever exported thence, under a single order, including all

the most esteemed machines then in use, for their contemplated purposes, together with workmen in turning, filing,
carding, spinning, dressing, weaving, &c. They have
continued to increase their machinery in number and value, and have not only constructed for themselves, but for
others. Among their efforts, we lately noticed 700 spindles, which they have completed for Mr. F. Rapp of E-
conomy, together with the necessary dressing and warping
machines, looms, &c.

Their establishment contains upwards of twenty seven
hundred spindles:—twenty two throstles of 84 spindles,
and six mules of 180 spindles each, together with the
necessary preparation machines; sixteen looms for weaving
yard wide sheetings, dresser, warper, &c. They produce
daily about seven hundred weight of yarn, from No. 5 to
22, and about four hundred and fifty yards of cotton cloth—
consuming about six hundred bales of cotton annually.—
They employ about one hundred and seventy persons, including those at work in their machine shop. The annual
value of their manufactured goods and machinery, is
100,000 dollars, calculating their yarns and sheetings at
the eastern prices, by which they usually are regulated.
The power, operating this machinery, is a steam engine of
about forty horse power, which turns also the lathes, grind-
stones, &c. of the machine shop, and forces the escape
steam through the building, diffusing a general and moderate heat.

Mr. JOHN M'ILROY,

In wood, between Front and Second streets, has in operation 80 hand looms, employed as follows :—

On 3-4 plaids,	62	producing 930 yards per day,	value	$152 20
On Stripes,	10	" 160 " " "	"	23 40
On Check,	8	" 112 " " "	"	19 04
Total looms,	80	producing 1202 yards per day.		$194 62

There is employed in the business of this concern, including the colouring department, 155 hands. The number
of yards manufactured per annum, is 363,600, and the
whole at 15 cts. per yard, amounts to 54,540 dollars. Mr.
M'Ilroy is making considerable additions to the number of
his looms. It is probable 200 will be in operation in a
short time.

Mr. JAMES SHAW,

In Wood street, between Sixth and Liberty, has in operation 52 hand looms, employed as follows :

On plaids, 30, producing 600 yards per day. value $84 00
On check, 22, " 444 " " " 74 80

Total looms, 52 producing 1044 yards per day. valued at $158 80

Mr. Shaw will increase the number of his looms this year considerably. The number of persons now in his employ is 70. The number of yards made annually, 234,000. Value, 35,100 dollars.

Mr. THOMAS GRAHAM,

In Market, between Fifth and Liberty streets, has 34 hand looms in operation, which are employed as follows :

On plaids, 18, producing 400 yds. per day, value, $56 00
On stripes, 6 " 120 " " " 16 80
On check, 8 " 144 " " " 24 48
On Wilmington stripe, 2 " 24 " " " 5 28

Total looms, 34 producing 688 " " value, 102 56

Forty-five hands are employed. The number of yards wove per year, 206,200, and their value, $30,930,00.

Messrs. TILFORD AND SONS,

Near Pittsburgh, have 8 looms employed on stripes, plaids, &c. They weave annually about 36,000 yards, besides a considerable quantity of cassinets and woollen carpeting. They employ about 15 hands, and the value of their manufacture is about 6123 dollars.

MISCELLANEOUS.

There are in Pittsburgh, besides those already enumerated, 47 looms, which are engaged in various kinds of weaving—such as coverlits, carpets, linen, cotton cloth, &c. Among all, 60 hands are engaged, weavers, spoolers, &c. who make per year, about 211500 yards of various stuffs, valued at 29,210 dollars.

6*

RECAPITULATION.

	looms.	*hands.*	*cot. spun.*	*wove.*		*value.*
Phœnix Factory,	16	170	210000 lb.	135000 yds. with machinery,		100000
Arthurs' do		13	13,500			4185
M'Ilroy's do	80	155		360000		54540
Shaw's do	52	70		234000		35100
Graham's do	34	40		206200		30930
Tilford's do	8	15		36000		6123
Miscellaneous	47	60		211500		29610
Totals,	237	523	223500	1,182,700		$ 260,488

It may be remarked, that the plaids, stripes, &c. produced at the above establishments, are of the best quality,
as to material, workmanship, and colours, and that they
can be afforded at a cheaper rate than they can be brought
from beyond the mountains.　They afford a convenient
and profitable employment to a great number of workmen,
many of whom have their shops attached to their own dwellings, and employ their own children in the preparatory
and lighter parts of the business.

The yarn for the hand looms is principally supplied by the
Phœnix Factory, and the Factory of the Messrs. Arthurs.
The remainder is procured from some of the Factories
named below, which we enumerate to complete the view of
the cotton business in this section of the country.

4. The Brownsville or Bridgeport Cotton Factory,
situated at Bridgeport, on the Monongahela, and owned by
Mr. Thomas Burk.　In this factory there are 750 spindles,
and about 500 lbs. yarn, from No. 13 to 18, is produced
per day.

5. The Economy Steam Cotton Factory, situated 17
miles below this city, owned by the Economists, is just
going into operation, with about 500 spindles, to be increased shortly to 1000.　Both spinning and weaving to
be carried on in this establishment.

6. The Beaver Cotton Factory, belonging to Messrs.
Pugh & Wilson, propelled by water power.　What quantity of goods it produces, we have not ascertained.

7. Steubenville Factory, owned by J. Sutherland & Co.
The machinery is propelled by steam—produces yarn only.

8. Another new factory, at the same place, owned by
Messrs. Larimore, Kalb & Co.—also propelled by steam
power.—Spinning and weaving carried on.　They have also
some hand looms employed upon chambrays, stripes, &c.

9. The Wheeling Cotton Factory, lately commenced by
a joint stock company, who have already 30,000 dollars

invested.—Steam power. Both spinning and weaving carried on in this factory.

WOOLLEN.

The manufactures of Pittsburgh in this branch, are as yet very limited, nor can we reasonably expect a great increase, considering the present duties on woollen stuffs that are imported, and the disposition usually predominant among all classes, to purchase foreign cloth. The principal article that is manufactured here, in this line, is cassinet—its cheapness and durability generally commanding a market.

JAMES ARTHURS & SONS,

In connection with their steam cotton factory, have a woollen establishment, where they have during the last year manufactured, carded and dressed, to wit:

Of broad cloth,	1200 yards. Aver. v. per yard $4			$4800
Of cassinets,	3600 '	'	' 85 cts.	3060
Yards,	4800			$7860

They carded and spun 15000 pounds of wool, and dressed 8000 yards of country cloth. Do all their own dressing, and employ in this branch 11 hands.

HEADRICK & GIBB,

Have a woollen manufactory at the corner of Liberty street and Diamond alley The machinery is put in motion by horse power, and their business for the last year, is as follows:—

2 looms on cassinets, 14 yds. per day, 4200 yds. at 85 cts.	$3570 00
Carded for country 7000 lb. wool at 6¼ cts.	437 50
1 loom on coverlits, carpets, &c.	700 00
Spun for country 3000 lbs.	
	$4707 50

The proprietors have met with considerable encouragement, and they will consequently make considerable additions this year. Seven hands are employed.

FLEECEDALE WOOLLEN MANUFACTORY,

Situated on Chartier's creek, a few miles west of Pittsburgh,
near the Steubenville road.   This is a respectable establishment, and is owned by Messrs. A. & J. MURPHY.
The machinery is driven by water power.   The business
of this establishment for the last year as follows—

Four looms on cassinets, 32 yards per day, 9600 yards.	$9600
One loom on broadcloth, 5 ' ' 1500 '	7500
	10,100 yds. $ 17100

There are two carding machines, and one mule of 90
spindles, by which 10,000 lbs. of wool has been carded and
spun.   Attached, is a Fulling mill and Dyeing establishment.   16 persons are employed.

The Messrs. Murphy's are among the first rate clothiers
in our country, who combine, with great enterprize and
industry, an indefatigable zeal to render their manufactures worthy of public support.   The specimens which
they have exhibited, from time to time, place their fabrics
in the most respectable light; and we doubt whether their
high-priced cloths have been surpassed by those of any of
our Domestic Manufactories, in finish, colour and texture.
Sorry, too, are we, that so much of our home manufactures
of this kind, which are so well deserving attention, should
still be in a manner superseded by the fabrics of Europe.

Fleecedale cloths and cassinets may be seen and purchased at M. S. Mason & M'Donough's wholesale dry
good store, Wood street.

RECAPITULATION.

	cloth.	cassinet.	value.	hands.
Messrs. Arthurs & Sons,	1200 yds.	3600 yds.	$7,860 00	11
Headrick & Gibb,		4200	3,570 00	7
do do cassinets, carpets, &c.			1,137 50	
A. & J. Murphy,	1500	9600	17100 00	16
	2,700	17,400 yds.	$ 29,667 50	34

There are also in the City, 4 stocking weavers, { 4000 00
whose work per year may be valued at

Making the total value of woollens made last year, $ 33,667 50 cents.

GLASS.

In the manufacture of this article, Pittsburgh and the surrounding country, enjoys an extensive reputation. It is needless for us to repeat what we have said before, as to the advantages we possess—let it suffice, when we say, that the west, at least this part of it, is secure against any competition elsewhere in this branch of business. The glass of Pittsburgh and the parts adjacent, is known and sold from Maine to New Orleans.—Even in Mexico they quaff their beverage from the beautiful white-flint of Messrs. Bakewell, Page & Bakewell of our city. Let it be recollected too, that at a recent exhibition of American Manufactures, by the Franklin Institute of Philadelphia, where specimens of the finest glass made in the United States were brought forward, the premium was awarded to the gentlemen we have just named.

Should the waters of the east and west ever be connected, glass, of itself, will be an object of immense trade. The importation of the article would be immediately superseded, and even the eastern manufactories would find a powerful competitor in our occidental transportation.

PITTSBURGH GLASS WORKS,

Are situate on the south side of the Monongahela, opposite the Point, and is now conducted by Mr. F. LORENZ. This concern was the first of the kind established in the western country. It was built as early as 1797, by Gen. O'Hara and Major Craig. For a few years their success seemed very doubtful—so much so, that the latter gentleman withdrew, and left Mr. O'Hara to make the best of what was then termed a *losing concern*. But the General, who had a happier knack of seeing a few years before him, and drawing deductions from the nature of things, than any of his cotemporaries, persevered with his glass house, made large additions, prospered, and conducted it until his death, in 1819. It has since been rented, and now its operations are very extensive. Within the last year there has been manufactured, viz:—

Window Glass,	7,500 boxes	valued at $31,000
Porter Bottles,	160 gross	1,440
Hollow Ware,	3160 dozen	4,424
		$36,864

Forty-eight hands are employed, and upwards of 250 souls are living at and supported by this establishment. The consumption of coal for the last 12 months was 70754 bushels, beside 600 cords of wood.

BAKEWELL, PAGE & BAKEWELL'S GLASS HOUSE,

Situated on Water street, above Grant. Was erected in 1811. This establishment is devoted entirely to the manufacture of white or flint glass, and has succeeded in producing the best specimens of this article ever made in the United States. The admiration of this glass is not confined merely to home observers, but the great amount of it that has been exported, testify the reputation it enjoys abroad; and there is scarcely a stranger visits Pittsburgh, who is not desirous of taking a peep at Bakewell's Glass House. Amidst all the depressions and general stagnations of trade of past days, the proprietors of this concern have manifested a steady, persevering and enterprising spirit, as honourable to themselves as their manufactures are creditable to our country.

Our limits will not permit us to note the numerous articles that are made at this manufactory—they embrace every thing in the glass line, of every price and of every grade of workmanship, from the most beautiful to the most plain and uncut. There are employed here 61 hands, 12 of whom are constantly engaged in engraving and ornamenting. 50,000 bushels of coal are consumed annually, and the value of glass made per year is about 45,000 dollars.

BIRMINGHAM GLASS WORKS,

Erected in the year 1812, by Messrs. SUTTON, WENDT & Co. but are now conducted by Messrs. Wendt, Encell, Impson and others. This establishment manufactures window glass and green hollow ware entirely, and has done, and is still doing an immense business. Birmingham glass has been transported to all parts of the Union, and has acquired much celebrity for its good quality. The owners are all actual workmen, hence their disposition, as well as their interest has always been to render their articles of the best kind. They employ 60 hands—consume 40,000 bushels of coal, and manufacture, annually, viz:—

Window Glass,	4,000 boxes	value, $16,000
Porter Bottles,	100 gross	900
Hollow Ware,	10,000 dozen	11,040
		$27 940

STOURBRIDGE GLASS WORKS,

Near the corner of Ross and Second streets, erected by Mr. JOHN ROBINSON, in 1823. Manufactures white or flint glass only. Some very beautiful, and highly finished articles have been produced at this establishment, and we take great pride in noticing it, not only because another manufactory is added to our list, but because it exhibits the confidence of the enterprizing owner, in daring to compete with the old and reputable white flint establishment we have before taken notice of.

Mr. Robinson employs 18 hands—consumes 18000 bushels of coal, and his glass made per annum is valued at 22,000 dollars.

RECAPITULATION.

	hands.	value.	coal.
Pittsburgh Glass Works,	84	$36,864	60,754
Birmingham	40	27,940	40,000
Bakewell's	61	45,000	30,000
Robinson's	18	22,000	18,000
hands,	203	$131,804	bushels 148,754

As the following establishments may be said to be in our immediate neighbourhood, and as Pittsburgh is generally the storehouse and market of their manufactures, we shall notice them :—

Bridgeport Glass-works, on the Monongahela, manufactures window glass and hollow ware to the amount of about 4000 boxes, valued at 16,000 dollars.

New Albany, on the same river at the mouth of Redstone, manufactures annually window glass and hollow ware to the amount of 4000 boxes—equal to 16,000 dollars.

New Boston, at Perryopolis on the Youghiogany, makes window glass and hollow ware, yearly, to the amount of 2,000 boxes, equal to 8,000 dollars.

Williamsport, on the Monongahela, makes window glass, &c. to the amount of 3,000 boxes, valued at 12,000 dollars.

Geneva works, owned by Mr. Gallatin, manufactures, yearly, about 4,000 boxes, valued at 16,000 dollars.

Total number of boxes, 17,000   value, $68,000
To which add Pittsburgh window and flint glass,   131,804

Total value, $199,804

PAPER.

The manufacture of Paper is carried on to a very great
extent in the western counties of Pennsylvania. In 1810
there were but two paper mills in this part of the state, the
oldest of which was the Redstone mill, near Brownsville.
Now there are *nine*, four of which are owned in this city;
besides two in the adjacent county of Jefferson, Ohio, one
of which is owned here, viz :—

ANCHOR STEAM PAPER MILL,

Owned by Mr. H. HOLDSHIP, situated in Pittsburgh, corner of Ross and Brackenridge streets.   This is the largest
paper making establishment west of the mountains.   It is
put into operation by an engine of 30 horse power and employs 88 hands.   There are 6 vats, which produce on an
average, the year round, 40 reams per week each, which
may be valued at 3 dollars per ream, making each vat to
produce 2080 reams per annum, valued at 6,240 dollars.
The whole number of reams produced per year, is 12,480,
valued at 37,440 dollars.

The quality of Mr. Holdship's paper is certainly of the
first order, as is sufficiently tested by his extensive sales
in the east, as well as in the west.   Within the last 18
months, 40,000 dollars worth of Spanish paper has been
made at his mill, for the South American market, and which
has been shipped thence.

PITTSBURGH STEAM PAPER MILL,

In the Northern Liberties, and owned by J. PATTERSON
& Co. is driven by an engine of 20 horse power, and has
3 vats.   This concern is not now in operation.

CLINTON STEAM PAPER MILL,

Situate at Steubenville, and owned by Mr. H. HOLDSHIP
of this city.   Has an engine of 30 horse power, and 4 vats,
produces annually 8320 reams, which may be valued at
24,960 dollars.

FRANKLIN PAPER MILL,

On Little Beaver, Beaver county; owned by Messrs.
CRAMER & SPEAR of this city, is driven by water power;

has 2 vats, and manufactures about 9000 dollars worth of various kinds of paper annually.

BIG BEAVER PAPER MILL,

At the Falls of Big Beaver; owned by Messrs. JOHNSTON & STOCKTON, of this city. Machinery is driven by water power; has 2 vats and will make annually about 10,000 dollars worth of paper of all kinds.

For the same reason that we noticed the adjacent Glass-works, we will mention the neighbouring Paper Mills.

The *Sewickly* Paper mill, Westmoreland county, owned by General Markle—3 vats—water power. Messrs. Allen & Grant, agents for this city.

The *Redstone* Paper mill, in Fayette county, owned by Messrs. Jackson & Sharpless—2 vats—water power.

The *Yough* Paper mill, Fayette county, owned by Mr. D. Rogers—2 vats—water power.

The *Ohio* Paper mill, on Little Beaver, owned by Messrs. Bever & Bowman—2 vats—water power.

The *Meadville* Paper mill, in Crawford county, owned by Mr. M'Gaw—2 vats—water power.

The *Mountpleasant* Paper mill, Jefferson county, Ohio, owned by Mr. Updegraff—2 vats—water power.

A new steam paper mill will be erected this summer, by Mr. George Hirst & Co. near the U. States Arsenal. Mr. Belknap is now engaged on the engine.

The estimated average value of the paper produced at each vat in the water mills, at 5000 dollars per year; and the rags used in each vat, at 50,000 lbs. Taking all the mills at this average rate, and estimating rags at 5 cents per lb. the paper manufactured in the mills enumerated would be worth 150,000 dollars, and the amount laid out in the country for rags, would not be less that $58,000.

----•◍◍•----

FLOUR, &c.

There are four Steam Grist Mills; three in the city, and one in Birmingham; all in operation.

THE PITTSBURGH STEAM MILL,

Situated at the corner of Water street and Redoubt alley;

7

was established in 1812, by Oliver Evans, and is now conducted by Mr. GEORGE EVANS. It runs three pair of burrs, and can manufacture every 12 hours about 24 bbls. of flour; making the number of barrels per year 7,000, which valued at 3 dollars per barrel, are worth 21,000 dollars.

To this mill there is attached an extensive Plough manufactory, also carried on by George Evans; where patent, half patent, hill-side, premium and common ploughs of all sizes, of the most excellent workmanship, are made.

ALLEGHENY STEAM MILL,

Situate near the Allegheny river, on Irwin's alley; was established some years since, by William Anderson, but is now owned by Mr. JOHN HERRON. It runs two pair of stones, which grind and chop every 12 hours about 240 bushels. Connected with this mill is the

ALLEGHENY STEAM SAW-MILL,

Also owned by Mr. Herron. It is capable of running either one or two saws; one, however, is constantly cutting, and will turn out from 2000 to 2500 feet of boards per 12 hours; making about 600,000 feet per annum. Boards are worth 6 dollars per 1000.

EAGLE STEAM MILL,

On the Monongahela river, at the mouth of Suke's run; was originally established by Mr. A. Beelen; now conducted by Mr. Henderson. Has two pair of burrs, one of which is generally employed on country work; about 3500 barrels of flour are made per year, besides chopping and grinding of various kinds.

There is attached to this establishment, an extensive nail factory, which in the department we have devoted to Naileries, was overlooked. There is one ton of nails manufactured here per day, making yearly, 600,000 pounds. Valued at 36,000 dollars—7 machines in operation.

BIRMINGHAM STEAM MILL,

Carried on by Sutton & Nicholson. Has 2 pair of burrs, and does country work altogether. There is connected with this concern, as we have before stated, an extensive establishment for turning, boring and grinding of iron, &c.

In all the mills and factories which we have noted under the head of "Flour, &c." there are 45 hands employed, and the value of their products annually, is about 72,000 dollars.

PITTSBURGH LINEN AND BAGGING FACTORY.

Mr. Wm. Sutcliff is engaged in the erection of a Linen and Cotton Bagging Manufactory, on Hay street, near the Allegheny river. The machinery will be driven by an engine of 10 horse power, now building by himself, and is calculated to manufacture 200 yards of linen, and 400 of bagging per day.

BRASS, TIN AND COPPER.

There are in Pittsburgh, four brass foundries, where are manufactured all kinds of articles in that line. One or two of them, however, are kept almost constantly employed in casting the necessary brass-work for steam machinery. 11 hands are employed.

In the Tinning business there are 11 separate establishments which employ about 65 hands, and manufacture about 44000 dollars worth of ware per year.

There are also in the city, 6 copper-smith shops, engaged in the manufacture of stills, kettles, pipes, &c. &c. 25 hands are employed—value of manufactures, 14,000 dollars.

SMITHERIES.

Black-smiths.—Within the limits of the corporation, there are 24 black-smith shops, which employ 115 persons.

Among these we must notice the establishment of Mr. WATERS, near Herron's steam mill, where there are made, weekly, 30 dozen of shovels and 6 dozen of axes—making per annum the enormous number of 18,720 shovels and 3744 axes. Twenty-seven hands are employed.

The whole value of work done at our various black-smitheries per annum, is about 47,000 dollars.

White-smiths.—There are also, *six white-smith shops*—devoted to the finer branches of iron work. Among these are the scale beam and balance manufactories of Thomas

Hazelton and Hugh Hazelton, (separate concerns) to which we would call the attention of the public, as producing some of the finest pieces of work of the kind we have ever seen—Mr. T. Hazelton's particularly, who also carries on the manufactory of wheel-irons, locks, &c. &c.

We must also notice here, in addition, the

BIRMINGHAM LOCK MANUFACTORY,

Of J. & J. Patterson, jr. where are manufactured, knob, rim, fine plate and Bambury Stock Locks, from 6 to 12 inches.—Also, Norfolk Thumb Latches and Bolts. These articles are equal to any imported. Eleven hands are are employed and about 1100 dozen of the articles manufactured annually—value 4950 dollars.

Mr. Tustin, at Soho, has an extensive whitesmith shop.

The whole number of hands employed is 45, and the value of work produced in all—23,000 dollars.

Gun-smiths.—Of these there are four.—They employ 6 hands and manufacture rifles generally, with, or without percussion locks—some very handsome ones have been made by Mr. Lennox, next door to the Post Office and Mr. Walker in Fifth street.

Silver-smiths.—There are eight silversmiths and watch repairers. Two of these establishments, however, are entirely devoted to the gold and silversmith business:— That of Mr. John S. Heald, nearly opposite the Post office and that of Mr. Lucky in Diamond alley, where all manner of gold and silver work is handsomely and tastefully executed. Thirteen hands are employed in all, and the value of manufactures about 12,500 dollars.

LEATHER.

There are in Pittsburgh and suburbs, 9 tanneries, owned by the following gentlemen: Messrs. Hays, Caldwell, Peters, Thompson, Brown, M'Caddon, Bayard, Sample & M'Ilhinny. 52 hands are employed, and 65,000 dollars worth of leather made per annum.

Saddleries.—Of these we have 8. The establishment of Mr. John Little, at the corner of Market and Water streets, is the most extensive and elegant we have ever seen. The arrangement and economy of the interior is certainly very genteel, and not surpassed by any similar concern in the eastern cities. 47 hands are employed.

Messrs. Hanson & Brice, and Plumer & Co. have very respectable saddleries—one at the corner of Market and Second and the other at the corner of Market and Third streets. They employ 27 hands.

In all the establishments 104 hands are employed, and the annual value of their manufactures is about $ 85,000.

Shoe and Boot-makers.—In this branch of business, Pittsburgh is very extensively engaged, and notwithstanding the immense number of boots and shoes made here per annum, there is not a sufficient quantity for the consumption of the town and country as is evident from the nume-rous shoe-stores in the city, that are filled with eastern manufactures, and the vast amount which they dispose of. There are 45 boot and shoe makers, who employ 225 hands and manufacture annually 95000 dollars worth of shoes and boots. The value of shoes vended by merchants, and at shoe stores, in no way connected with their manufacture, is about 35,000 dollars per annum.

WOOD.

The excellence of our timber and the various kinds that are found in this region of country, present materials for the manufacture of all kinds of articles in wood.

Chair-makers.—Of these there are six, whose products are of the most elegant kind. Their ornamenting particularly, being very creditable to our artists—30 hands are employed, and the value of work done per annum, about 12,000 dollars.

Cabinet-makers.—There are 14 cabinet-makers in the city, who employ 65 hands, and make about 45,000 dollars worth of furniture per annum.

Sending to the east for cabinet furniture as has been done by some of our citizens, is absurd as well as ungene-rous towards our own workmen. The work that has been turned out of our shops, is equal to any made in Phil-adelphia or elsewhere.

Coach-makers.—Of these there are but 2, who are suffici-ent for the business done here in that line. A number of very

7*

handsome stages, gigs and sulkys have been made during the last year. 15 hands are employed—value of work, 10,000 dollars.

Wagon and plough-makers.—There are 7 establishments where wagons and ploughs of a dozen different kinds are made—employ 35 hands, and manufacture per year to the amount of 12,000 dollars.

Wheel-rights.—Of these there are but two, who make spinning wheels, hatter's blocks, &c. &c.—Employ seven hands—value of work, 3000 dollars per annum.

Carpenters.—There are now upwards of 260 persons engaged in this branch of business, and it is probable owing to the extensive buildings going on this summer many more will be employed. We are unable to come at the value of their work.

Boat-building.—In this branch there are upwards of 140 persons engaged in the various departments. The value of steam boats, keel boats, barges, &c. built last year, amounted to 62,000 dollars.

Plane-makers.—There are three shops of this kind in the city, which beside making a sufficient number of planes for the home market, supply a great portion of the western country.

Last-making.—Mr. Fosdick is the only person we know, who is engaged in this branch; in which he does a respectable business.

BRICK AND STONE.

There are seven extensive brick yards in the suburbs, where, during the last year, 4,500,000 bricks were made. From the early commencement our brickmakers have made this season, and the activity of all hands, there will be, no doubt, double the quantity made this year. There are employed, 100 persons. Bricks are valued at $3 50 cents per 1000.

We have five stone cutting establishments, where all things in the stone line are made, from a mullar to a monument. 16 hands are employed—value of work per year 12,000 dollars.

POTTERIES.

Of these there are three; one in the city and two in the suburbs.—The first is Mr. F. Freeman's, who manufactures, besides earthen ware, a considerable quantity of stone ware and fire bricks. Employs 4 hands—value of ware, &c. made per year, about 2000 dollars.

Birmingham Pottery.—Owned by Mr. James Barr; employs 8 hands, and made last year 36 kilns of ware, the exact value of which at wholesale prices is 2980 dollars 80 cents. Mr. Barr will probably commence the manufacture of stone ware this summer.

Allegheny Pottery.—Conducted by Mr. Heckesweller; employs two hands, and manufactures about 1200 dollars worth of ware annually.

ROPE WALK.

Mr. John Irwin in Allegheny town, has an extensive rope factory, where cordage of all kinds, from the smallest wrapping twine, to the largest ship cables are made. 14 hands are employed, and 15,000 dollars worth made annually.

His warehouse is in Pittsburgh, at the corner of Liberty and Fourth streets.

WHITE LEAD.

There are three establishments in the city which manufacture this article.

AVERY & Co's. WHITE LEAD FACTORY,

In Penn, between Hand and Wayne streets; was established some years since, by James S. Stevenson; and manufactures about 3000 kegs per annum.

BRACKENRIDGE & PORTER'S WHITE LEAD FACTORY,

Near the corner of Sixth and Liberty streets, was built last year, and is in very successful operation. Makes 2400 kegs per year.

BRUNOT'S WHITE LEAD FACTORY,

Situate a short distance above the Catholic Chapel. Manufactures 1200 kegs per annum.

The whole number of kegs made annually, is 6,600—wholesale price is 3 dollars 50 cts. per keg. Making the total value of white lead made per annum, 23,100 dollars.

DISTILLERIES & BREWERIES.

There are four distilleries in the city; two of which are principally employed in rectifying:—

Among these we must not forget the establishment of our very particular friend Mr. GEORGE SUTTON, who is the manufacturer of the celebrated *Tuscaloosa*, which has been drunk from Maine to Georgia, and which is so highly esteemed in the southern states, for its *anti-miasmatic* and *animalculae-destroying* qualities; for the mildness with which it *insurges* the consumer; and for the fresh and exhilerated spirits that it gives to those who may have been accidentally rendered *obsolete* by its power, when the returning rays of *translucence* break upon them. Mr. Sutton has been very successful in the manufacture and sale of this liquor. Orders from all parts are daily arriving. Mr. S. has devoted much time and attention to this business, so much so, that he is now engaged in making a new beverage as a competitor of the Tuscaloosa, to which he has given the inspiring and beautiful name of the " *Pure Rock Water,*" or in the language of the last of the Mohicans, the " *Real Tallyvally Cord.*" This is an admirable liquor; blending with the mildness of milk all the sparkling vivacity of champaign. It steals gently upon the senses, like music upon the soul, and animates the intellect without ever *collapsing* an idea.

Breweries.—Of these establishments there are three. The oldest and most extensive is the *Point Brewery* conducted by Mr. Shiras. Manufactured last year 2500 barrels of porter and 1500 barrels of beer. Value, 17,000 dollars.

Mr. George Shiras, jr. will erect this summer near the Point, an extensive brick brewery, which will be capable of manufacturing 5000 barrels of beer and porter annually.

The *Pittsburgh Brewery*, which was consumed by fire last winter, is now rebuilding with brick, and enlarged.— Several brewings have already been made. There will be made at this concern during the present year, about 2000 barrels of porter and 1200 barrels of beer. Valued at 13,600 dollars. The brewery is owned by Messrs. Brown and Varner, and is situated on Liberty, near the head of Market street.

Kensington Brewery.—Conducted by Messrs. COLLART & SILVEY. Manufacture about 600 barrels of porter and ale, and 1,500 barrels of beer—value 7,500 dollars.

In the whole number of distilleries and breweries, 40 hands are employed, and the total value of spirits and malt liquor distilled, rectified and brewed, is $48,000.

PRINTING & BOOK-BINDING.

There are in Pittsburgh, eight Printing Offices, two of which are altogether devoted to book and job printing, the remainder are newspaper establishments, viz:

The "*Pittsburgh Gazette,*" the first paper printed in the western country; was established by John Scull, Esq. in 1783. It is of imperial size; is now conducted and owned by Messrs. D. & M. MACLEAN, and is one of the most respectable and ably conducted weekly journals in Pennsylvania.

The *Statesman*, a weekly paper, also of imperial size; was first published as the "*Commonwealth,*" by E. Pentland, in 1805, and after having passed through the hands of numerous owners, is now conducted by Messrs. ANDREWS & WAUGH. This paper is at this time in a more flourishing condition than it has been for many years, owing to the late improvement of its appearance and the addition to the editorial department.

The "*Mercury,*" a super royal paper, published once a week; was commenced by JAMES C. GILLELAND in 1810, from whom it was purchased by the present editor, JOHN M. SNOWDEN.

The "*Pittsburgh Recorder,*" also a weekly super-royal paper; was established by the Rev. Mr. ANDREWS, in 1821 and is devoted to religion and miscellany.

The "*Allegheny Democrat*," printed on an imperial sheet; was established in 1823; and is owned and edited by JOHN M'FARLAND.

Book-binderies.—Of these there are three; one belonging to Messrs. CRAMER & SPEAR; one to Messrs. JOHNSTON & STOCKTON, and one to Mr. JOHN S. SHELDON. These establishments have machines, by which ledgers and account books may be ruled to any given pattern.

In the different printing offices and binderies, there are 46 hands engaged.

———◆———

TOBACCO.

In the manufacture of this article there are 11 establishments; which produce annually, about 4,833 kegs of tobacco, and about 4000000 of Segars—140 hands are employed :—value of manufactures, 53,000 dollars.

———◆———

WIRE WEAVING.

There are two establishments engaged in the manufacture of sieves, fenders, &c. and the weaving of wire. At one of these (Mr. Townsend's,) wheat fans are made in a very superior manner. Six hands are employed in all, and 10,000 dollars worth of work made annually.

———◆———

SALT.

It is an astonishing fact, that notwithstanding the numerous salinous indications that for many years were known to exist about Pittsburgh, no one until within a year or two past, ever made an attempt to obtain salt water by boring. We almost feel ashamed of ourselves, when we look back at the time when salt was commanding 12 and 14 dollars per barrel, while inexhaustible supplies of saline water, were running a few hundred feet below us.

Mr. George Anshutz, at the mouth of Saw-mill run, on the Ohio, one mile below the Point, succeeded in obtaining water of an excellent quality, at between 1 and 2 hundred feet. This water is raised by a small steam engine, and emptied into two large pans which are kept constantly boiling, together with several refining kettles. 50 bushels of salt are made per day, amounting yearly, to about 4000 barrels :—valued at 5000 dollars.

Mr. Boyle Irwin, at the mouth of Nine-mile run, on the Monongahela, has also a well of very strong water; has one pan in operation, and makes 25 bushels per day, or about 2000 bushels per annum :—value 2500 dollars.

Mr. M'Donald, at Chartiers creek, on the Steubenville road, a few miles from the city, has an excellent well with one pan, and makes about 25 bushels per day.

Mr. Thomas Neel, on the Monongahela, above the mouth of Turtle creek, has tolerable good water, and manufactures a considerable quantity—we are not aware of the amount.

Mr. William C. Miller is now boring on the north side of the Allegheny, two miles above Pittsburgh—water has been found but not of sufficient strength as yet. A steam engine for pumping, and pans, &c. are already put up.

Mr. Anshutz talks of boring this summer immediately in the city, near Grant's hill. Several gentlemen have wells under way in the vicinity.

On the Conemaugh and Kiskeminitas rivers, about 40 miles from Pittsburgh, there are twenty-five salt manufactories in operation. Among all, 58 pans are in use, which make daily 1550 bushels of salt, or 310 barrels.

Of all these works now in blast, twenty-four are on the Kiskeminitas, situated within three miles of each other, and within the same space 10 new wells were under way, but which with a great many others, owing to the present low price of salt, have not been gone on with.

These establishments give employment to at least 400 persons, and support, including managers, coopers, blacksmiths, colliers, boilers, &c. and their families, from 10 to 1200 souls.

So much has been said in various public communications, on the subject of salt manufacture, and its importance to us as a trading commodity, that further remark may be deemed useless. We will only say, that the great competition that exists in the western country, will continue to keep the price of salt so low, that no very great advantage can arise from its manufacture, and nothing but a canal through the interior of Pennsylvania, a communication by water with Lake Erie, or a cessation of the salt works on the Kenhawa, will cause our salt to find a *profitable* market. The price of the article is only 1 dollar 25 cts. per barrel.

Miscellaneous Manufactories, &c.

Besides the manufactories heretofore noted, there are the following:--1 Sickle maker, 3 Brush makers, 7 Hatters, 2 Dyers, 11 Painters and Glaziers, 11 Plasterers, 12 Coopers, 44 Tailors, 8 Bakers, 4 Confectioners, 1 Organ maker, 1 Button maker, 2 Saddle-tree makers and platers, 2 Chemists, 5 Chandlers, 1 Comb maker, 2 Reed makers, 4 Turners in wood, 2 Sash makers, 1 Rigger, 2 Bellows makers, 3 Pattern makers, 2 Cutlers and 1 Tackle-block-maker. Among the whole of these, 310 hands are employed, and the value of their work per annum, is valued at 135,000 dollars.

Jappaning.—Mr. WHITEHOUSE, in Kensington, carries on the jappaning business, and has exhibited to us some very handsome specimens of his art, on iron, tin, copper, and wood. He also manufactures tea and bread trays of *machee* paper, some of which are very beautiful, and well deserving of public attention.

New Cotton Manufactory.—We omitted under the head of "Cotton," to state that Mr. Robinson, an English gentleman, will shortly commence the erection of a cotton manufactory on the west side of the Allegheny, immediately below the bridge.

In the conclusion of our statistical account of the manufactures of Pittsburgh, we cannot refrain from congratulating our fellow citizens on the important attitude they are assuming, and the great additions and improvements that are daily making, in the various branches—and we think that the following recapitulation of our whole manufacturing concerns, will be highly gratifying, as exhibiting the immense value that is attached to the labour, skill and industry of our artizans.

GRAND RECAPITULATION OF MANUFACTURES.

Iron	$559,000
Nails	309,000
Castings	132,610
Steam Engines	152,800
Cotton	200,488
Woollen	83,667
Glass	131,804
Paper	82,400
Brass, Tin and Copper ware	73,000
Smithwork and other metallic manufactures	82,000
Wood work	177,000
Spiritous and Malt Liquors	60,000
Flour	36,000
Boards, Brick and Stone	37,500
Leather, Shoes, and Saddlery	236,000
Potteries	6,180
Ropes,	15,000
Tobacco, Segars and Snuff	53,000
Wire Work	10,000
Salt	8,000
White Lead	23,100
Miscellaneous manufactures	135,000
Total	**$ 2,553,549**

In the various branches of the mechanic arts above enumerated, there are 2,997 persons employed.

ALLEGHENY COUNTY.

The following is a correct statement of the number of Mills, Distilleries, &c. in Allegheny county.

Grist-mills	79
Saw-mills	65
Distilleries	130
Tanyards	21
Carding Machines	10
Fulling-mills	13
Oil and Chopping Mills	15

The Grist-mills, beside supplying our semi-weekly markets with about 322,000 lbs. or 16,100 bbls. of flour, furnish our merchants with about 45,000 barrels annually.

The Distilleries yield, in the same time, about 125,000 gallons of whiskey.

8

COMMERCE.

The commercial and trading transactions of Pittsburgh, during the last 12 months, have far surpassed those of any former period. The vast increase of population and the consequent demand for the various necessaries of life; the extensive range of country that is supplied from our city, and the facilities which are afforded for transportation by our numerous streams and turnpike roads, combined with the spirit and enterprize of our merchants, are the great causes of our prosperity. Our extensive manufacturing and mercantile concerns, must remain unrivalled in the western country, as to their locality and advantageous position. While we are supplying the west and the south, with iron, nails, glass, whiskey, paper, cottons, castings, &c. &c. we are supplying the north with dry goods, groceries and all kinds of merchandize, and the east with linen, feathers, beeswax, bacon, lard, flour, and a variety of domestic products. To every point around us, the trade of Pittsburgh extends. She is as it were the central spot of the great western trading concern. But it may be here observed, that although we have been, and are progressing very rapidly in every department of business, our increase is nearly balanced by the indulgence of our citizens in foreign luxuries and superfluities. The balance of trade is very small in favour of Pittsburgh, considering the means she has of monopolizing trade and realizing wealth; and it admits of a doubt, whether we will be any richer five years to come, than we now are, if our imports of foreign goods be proportionate to the supposed increase of our manufacturing and other domestic concerns.

If we wish to increase our manufacturing interests; encourage them by purchasing their fabrics. It is in this way that a competition must be excited, which together with the duties already laid, will so far supersede the importation of such foreign goods as we can make ourselves Then the balance of trade would not only be found in Pittsburgh to a great amount, but throughout our common country.

The following account of the imports into our city, for the last year, ending first of April, has been obtained by a great deal of labour and pains. When we say imports, we must be understood, as meaning all those articles which are brought over the mountains, to wit:—

IMPORTS.

Merchandize of various kinds,	$1,232,000
Groceries and Liquors,	813,000
Drugs, Stationary, &c.	74,000
Total,	$2,119,000

Of the Groceries, $339,000 were domestic, and of the Merchandize, 425,000.

The amount of sales made during the same period of the imports, were as follows:

Merchandize of all kinds,	$932,000
Groceries and Liquors,	801,000
Drugs, Stationary, &c.	62,000
	$1,795,000
Leaving on hand,	324,000
	$2,119,000

Of the sales made, $22,465 were books—and $179,500 sold at auction.

The following is a tolerably correct statement of our exports for one year, ending on the first of April last:

EXPORTS.

Iron	$398,000
Nails	210,000
Castings	88,000
Steam Engines	100,000
Cotton Yarns and Cloths	160,324
Glass	105,000
Paper	55,000
Porter	18,000
Flour	10,500
Tobacco and Segars	25,800
Wire Work	8,000
Axes, Scythes, Shovels, Sickles, &c.	49,000
Whiskey, 4,200 bbls. at 22 cts. per gal.	29,832
Bacon, 860,000 lbs.	51,820
Dry Goods, &c. exported to the north and west	480,000
Groceries and Foreign Liquors ditto ditto	525,000
Saddlery, and other manufactures in Leather	236,000
White Lead	17,000
Miscellaneous exports of Beeswax, Feathers, Candles, Soap, Cordage, Coal, Country Linen, Cider, Apples, &c.	214,000
Total	$2,781,276
Leaving a balance of trade in our favor, of	662,276

In relation to the trade in Salt, and Lumber, a very extensive business is done. During the past year, there were inspected and sold in Pittsburgh, 13,739 barrels of salt, amounting to $17,173.

In the same period, 3,163, 690 feet of boards were measured, which, together with a large quantity of shingles, scantling, laths, logs and hewn timber, were purchased at about 22,818 dollars. Upon these articles our salt and lumber merchants have realized a profit of about $11,500.

CARRYING TRADE.

Whatever may be the importance of canals, or rail roads, or any mean of internal transportation between Pittsburgh and the Atlantic, it was highly injudicious to represent our carrying trade as amounting far beyond what it really is. During the late session of the Legislature, it was stated that 900,000 dollars had been paid yearly for carriage, in Pittsburgh. We certainly are not inimical to canals, but when great questions involving the interests of the state as well as its credit, are agitated, it is improper for the purpose of carrying a popular measure, or to answer the views of a few, to misrepresent that which is the most important data upon which the benefits of an artificial navigation can be decided.

From the first of April 1825, to the first of April 1826, 3460 wagons passed the turnpike gate. Averaging their weight of goods at 4000 pounds each, the whole weight of goods transported, would amount to 13,840,000 pounds. Allowing three cents per pound, as the price of carriage, which is probably something higher than the general average would bear; the whole amount of carriage paid during the last year, would be 415,200 dollars The amount paid for return carriages during the same period, was about 103,800 dollars, making the total amount of carriages hitherward and hence, 504,015 dollars.

It is certain that the amount of goods brought to Pittsburgh during the past 12 months, was greater than that of any former period; and although the price of carriages falls far short of what it was stated to have been, $395,985, still the sum actually paid is enormous, and is sufficient of itself to warrant the investment of monies in the great system of internal improvement, now progressing in Pennsylvania.

NAVIGATION.

On this subject we cannot do more than recall to the re-collection of our fellow citizens, the unexampled bustle and activity exhibited on our wharves, during the past spring, and the immense shipping business done by our commission merchants. It is probable our steam boat proprietors have never before had such a long series of profitable running in one season. In fact, the continued high waters—the immense quantity of freight daily arriving, and the nume-rous travellers that are ever passing and repassing, seems to have given a new and astonishing impulse to our navi-gation. From three till eight steam boats have been con-stantly in port, notwithstanding the *head* of navigation is 90 miles below us, as our Wheeling friends would have it.

There arrived at the port of Pittsburgh, during the past year, 70 steam boats, and the number of departures 78.

The number of keel boats that have arrived and depar-ted in the same period. amounts to 470, and the flats to one hundred and forty-five.

The whole amount of tonnage employed in our naviga-tion, for the last year, was 17525 tons. The arrivals of tons of actual freight, consisting of the products of the west and south, cotton, tobacco, sugar, molasses, hemp, &c. &c. was, 7,190, The departure of tons, of actual freight—such as merchandize and Pittsburgh manufactures, was 15,250.

Taking the distance from the head of the Ohio to the highest navigable point of the Mississippi, then adding the distances to the same points on the various streams that empty into these two rivers, together with the distance from the mouth of the Ohio, to New Orleans, and there is presented an uninterrupted line of navigation of upwards of 17,000 miles. Upon this vast extent of water commu-nication, there are now, about 95 steam boats, and innu-merable other water craft employed.

STEAM BOATS.

THERE are few places in the west that have entered into any thing like successful competition with Pittsburgh, in the building of steam boats. Cincinnati is the only

8*

town that may be considered as a rival.—And as to her, it would not be the fault of her public writers or boat-own-ers, if the fame of the few good vessels they have con-structed, was not known, instantaneously, from one end of the river to the other. The Cincinnati folks ap-pear to be an extremely jealous people; they examine our Pittsburgh boats with as much scrutiny as a broker would a well executed counterfeit note; their remarks too, are communicated with as little regard to number, manner, and brevity as possible, while, at the same time, they have no objections whatever to ingraft our improvements on their *very costly* machinery. We must confess, that as to matters of *finish* and *decoration*, we do not, at all times, equal the "*Queen of the West;*" but that is, because we do not choose to spend as much money as they do in that way. What money we have to spare, is principally put in the hulls and machinery of our steam vessels, and the effect is amply attested by the manner in which they generally make headway. And if we have not been misinformed, the Pittsburgh boats have, *sometimes,* been able to shew themselves as rather *better* than *second best.*

But, jesting apart, and to speak *modestly,* we do say it, who probably ought not so to do, that our steam boats are, take them one and all, the best on the western waters, their *Paragons, Pioneers,* and *Cavaliers,* to the contrary notwithstanding.

The first steam boat that ever floated on the Ohio and Mississippi, was the *New Orleans,* of 400 tons, built at Pittsburgh, in 1812, by Mr. Fulton, of New-York. She ran between N. Orleans and Natchez for about two years, when she was wrecked near Baton Rouge.

Since the year 1812, the following boats have been built here, and in the immediate neighbourhood :

COMET	75 tons	RAPID	150 tons.
Vesuvius	390	Western Engineer	50
Ætna	390	Superior	60
Buffaloe	300	Neville	120
James Monroe	90	Pitt. & St. L. Pack.	133
Franklin	125	Pittsburgh	133
Oliver Evans	75	Rambler	150
Harriett	40	Henry Baldwin	40
New Orleans	300	Phœnix	150
Geo. Madison	200	Eclipse	200
Gen. Jackson	200	Herald	130
James Ross	300	Friendship	180

Frankfort	220	President	250
Tamerlane	220	La Fayette	200
Rising States	150	Gen. Brown	250
Olive Branch	300	Wm. Penn	150
Cumberland	250	Bolivar	250
Favorite	250	Gen. Wayne	250
Dolphin	150	Paul Jones	250
Expedition	150	De Witt Clinton	198
Telegraph	150	Messenger	160
Decatur	75	Commerce	195
Liberator	250	Gen. Coffee	150
Hercules	150	Pocahontas	200

Making the whole number of boats 48, and their tonnage 8,624. They cost, in all, about $ 495,000.

There are to be built this summer, in and about Pittsburgh, 5 additional steam boats: 2 at Phillips & Graham's on the Ohio, of 250 tons each—2 at the Point, each of 190 tons, and 1 at Suke's run of 196 tons.

Corporations and Institutions.

BANKS.

Bank of Pittsburgh—Corner of Market and Third sts. Incorporated in 1814. Notes for discount must be offered on Tuesday.

President—JOHN DARRACH. *Cashier*—ALEX. JOHNSTON, Jr.

Branch Bank of the U. States—Second, between Market and Ferry streets. Notes for discount must be handed in on Wednesday.

President—A. BRACKENRIDGE. *Cashier*—JAMES CORREY.

THE PITTSBURGH MANUFACTURING ASSOCIATION.

THIS institution was formed for the purpose of buying and selling, receiving, forwarding and disposing of, on commission, all articles of American produce and manufacture. It was commenced by a few of the mechanics and manufacturers of this city, by subscription, to a joint stock, divided into shares of twenty-five dollars each, payable in manufactured articles, of which about 4000 dollars were paid in, about the first of April, 1819, when a board of managers was appointed, and Geo. Cochran, of R'd. appointed Agent.

The business at first, was chiefly confined to bartering and exchanging; no profit was realized the first year, but a favourable report was made by the committee of investigation, and a vote of approbation passed on the conduct of the agent. In 1820, more shares were subscribed, amounting to 400, or 10,000 dollars in all; an act of incorporation was obtained for ten years, limiting the capital stock to 30,000 dollars.—The following conditions were prescribed;—" that a share shall always be 25 dollars, payable in gold or silver, or such articles as such subscribers shall be actually engaged in fabricating, and that no person or persons shall be permitted to subscribe to the capital stock, but such as are actually engaged in the business of domestic manufatures."

The mercantile affairs of the Association are conducted by nine managers, elected annually; no more than one third of whom can be re-elected.

The Stockholders of the Association, meet on the first Tuesdays of February, May, August, and November, annually. At their meetings, the bye-laws are enacted and committees appointed to investigate and report the proceedings of the managers, and conduct of the agent, every six months.

For the government of the Stockholders in their quarterly meetings, a President, Secretary and Treasurer, are elected annually.

In elections no votes of proxy are received, one share gives one vote, and no stockholder can be entitled by any greater number of shares, to more than four votes.

No dividend can be declared until after a contingent fund of 10 per cent. over the capital stock has been realized.

The business of 1820, yielded a dividend of 5 per cent. The depreciation on the relative value and reduction of prices of domestic manufactures in 1822–23, prevented any dividend being declared, the nominal profits being applied to reduce the prices of goods on hand. In 1823, a dividend of 5 per cent. was declared ; since that time a dividend of 10 per cent. per annum, has been declared : the capital and business of the association has greatly increased, and instead of bartering, the principal sales are for cash. The sales of Pittsburgh manufactures through this house alone, amount to 60,000 dollars per annum, and are increasing.

Manufacturers will find in this association faithful agents for the disposal of their goods, their object being to promote and encourage the spirit of domestic industry, by facilitating the intercourse between the merchant and the mechanic.

President—JOHN HANNEN.

Managers.

THOMAS HAZELTON,
JOHN MARSHALL,
THOMAS FAIRMAN,
ALEXANDER MILLER, jr.
JOHN SHERIFF,

JOHN SPEAR,
BENJ. BAKEWELL,
JAMES ARTHURS, jr.
THOMAS LIGGETT.

Secretary—S. R. JOHNSTON.
Treasurer—ABNER UPDEGRAFF.
Agent—GEORGE COCHRAN, of R'd.

INDEPENDENT BENEFICIAL SOCIETY.

Was formed in 1823, and incorporated in 1824. The object of this society, is the relief of such of its members as may become sick or disabled. Contributions are made monthly, which constitute the relief fund. Meet on the first Wednesday of every month. Elections are held annually, on the 11th of June. Initiation fee, $2.

President—Conrad Upperman. *Stewards*—James Sanderson and William Love. *Secretary*—S. Jones. *Treasurer*—John Snyder. *Messenger*—Samuel Mackey.

ERIN BENEVOLENT SOCIETY.

This institution was formed some years since, for the relief of distressed Irishmen. Their charities are still dispensed with Irish liberality.

President—Michael Allen. *Vice*—Henry Holdship. *Secretary*—Hugh Macshane. *Treasurer*—Webb Closey.

APPRENTICES' LIBRARY ASSOCIATION.

Was instituted in 1824, for the express purpose of improving the minds of the numerous apprentices in our city. The number and titles of the books of the association, are very respectable.

President—Thomas Bakewell. *Secretary*—David Maclean. *Librarian*—William Eichbaum, Sr.

MASONIC.

There are in Pittsburgh, besides a Royal Arch Chapter, three Lodges of A. Y. Masons. Their Hall is on Water, near the corner of Ferry street. There is also a Lodge at Lawrenceville.

ROYAL ARCH CHAPTER, NO. 113.

SHEPLY R. HOLMES, M. E. H. P.
ALBA FISK, M. E. K.
ARCHIBALD SHAW, S.
EDWARD J. ROBERTS, Recorder,
WILLIAM GRAHAM, Jr. Treasurer.

Stated meetings on the first Monday of every month.

LODGE NO. 45.

JOSHUA E. CROSBY, W. M.
PEREGRINE JOHNSTON, S. W
JESSE TAYLOR, J. W.
ROBERT CHRISTY, Secretary,
ARCHIBALD SHAW, Treasurer.

Stated meetings, the last Wednesday in every month.

OHIO LODGE, NO. 113.

EDWARD J. ROBERTS, W. M.
PATRICK M'KENNA, S. W.
ALFRED LOYD, J. W.
SAMUEL PETTIGREW, Secretary,
JOHN GALLAGHER, Treasurer.

Stated meetings, second Wednesday in every month.

MILNOR LODGE, NO. 165.

JOHN S. RIDDLE, W. M.
JAMES SHIDLE, S. W.
GEORGE W. JACKSON, J. W.
WILLIAM PENTLAND, Secretary,
GEORGE FARIS, Treasurer.

Stated meetings, third Wednesday of every month.

HAMILTON LODGE, NO. 173,
LAWRENCEVILLE.

W. W. FETTERMAN, W. M.
DUNNING R. M'NAIR, S. W.
ALEXANDER PENTLAND, J. W.
JOHN H. RICHARDSON, Secretary,
SAMUEL GARRISON, Treasurer.

Stated meeting, first Wednesday in every month.

MILITARY.

There are six independent Companies in the city : one of Dragoons; one of Artillery; one of Riflemen, and three of Infantry. The whole composing the " Pittsburgh Legion."

FIRE.

Our city, besides possessing an excellent Hose establishment, has four Fire Engines, viz. The *Eagle, Vigilant, Allegheny* and *Neptune.* They are all manned with full and spirited companies, and are in complete order.

There are many other institutions, in Pittsburgh, of a public nature, such as Sunday-school, bible, tract, and female benevolent societies. But our limits will not permit us to particularize.

Civil Officers of Allegheny County.

CHARLES SHALER,

President Judge of the Court of Common Pleas, and Quarter Sessions of the 5th judicial district.

Associate Judges—FRANCIS M'CLURE and JAMES RIDDLE.

Deputy Attorney General—ROSS WILKINS.

Prothonotary—WILLIAM M'CANDLESS.]

Register and Recorder—MATHEW STEWART.

Sheriff—WILLIAM LECKY.

Commissioners—D. COON, JOHN WILSON & JOHN PATTERSON.

Clerk to Commissioners—DAVID DRENNAN.

Treasurer—WILLIAM BLAIR.

Clerk of the Quarter Sessions and Orphan's Court—WM. PENTLAND.

Clerk of Mayor's Court—SILAS ENGLES.

Notaries Public.

JOHN THAW—*At Bank of U. States.*
M. B. LOWRIE—*West side of the Diamond.*
JOHN SNYDER—*At Bank of Pittsburgh.*

Constables.

JAMES MACKEY,   JOHN YOUNG,
CONRAD UPPERMAN,   JOHN MOORE.

COURTS.

United States' Court, for the Western District of Pennsylvania.

Judge—HON. WILLIAM WILKINS, Esq.

District Attorney—ALEXANDER BRACKENRIDGE, Esq.

Marshal—HUGH DAVIS, Esq.

Clerk—EDWARD J. ROBERTS, Esq.

Holds its Session semi-annually, in the City of Pittsburgh, on the first Monday of May, and the third Monday of October. And at Williamsport in Lycoming County, on the first Monday of June and October.

SUPREME COURT.

The Supreme Court of Pennsylvania, for the Western District, composed of the counties of Somerset, Westmoreland, Fayette, Greene, Washington, Allegheny, Beaver, Butler, Mercer, Crawford, Erie, Warren, Venango, Armstrong, Cambria, Indiana, and Jefferson, holds one term annually at Pittsburgh, on the first Monday of September to continue four weeks, if necessary.

WILLIAM TILGHMAN, *Chief Justice.*

THOMAS DUNCAN,
JOHN B. GIBSON,
THOMAS BURNSIDES, } *Associates.*
CHARLES HUSTON,

SAMUEL GORMLY, *Prothonotary.*

COURTS OF COMMON PLEAS, &c

Courts of Common Pleas, Quarter Sessions of the Peace, and Orphans' Court, for the 5th District of Pennsylvania, are held as follows, *viz:*—For the county of Beaver, on the 2d Mondays of January and April, the 4th Monday of August, and the 3d Monday of October. —For the county of Butler, on the 1st Mondays of January, April, July, and October—and for the county of Allegheny, on the 3d Mondays of January and April, and the 1st Mondays of August and November.

MAYOR'S COURT.

The Mayor's Court for the City of Pittsburgh, is held on the 2d Mondays of February and May, and 4th Mondays of July, and October.

List of Attorneys,

Practising at the Pittsburgh Bar, and resident in Pittsburgh, arranged agreeably to seniority of admission.

JAMES ROSS,
HENRY BALDWIN,
WALTER FORWARD,
JOHN M'DONALD,
NEVILLE B. CRAIG,
SAMUEL KINGSTON,
JAMES M. RIDDLE,
ALEX. BRACKENRIDGE,
EDWARD J. ROBERTS,
HARMAR DENNY,
RICHARD BIDDLE,
JAMES S. CRAFT,
SAMUEL A. ROBERTS,
ROSS WILKINS,
GEORGE WATSON,
TREVANION B. DALLAS,

BENJAMIN R. EVANS,
A. S. T. MOUNTAIN,
EPHRAIM PENTLAND,
WILLIAM ANDERSON,
W. W. FETTERMAN,
ROBERT BURKE,
CHARLES VON BONNHORST,
SAMUEL GORMLY,
EDWARD SIMPSON,
ROBERT WATSON,
CHARLES H. ISRAEL,
WILLIAM SNOWDEN,
ISAAC MURPHY,
JOHN GLENN,
CHARLES COOLMAN,
J. E. WAUGH.

List of Physicians.

The following gentlemen are practising physicians in our City.

Drs. BRUNOT,
MOWRY,
HOLMES,
CHURCH,
AGNEW,
GAZZAM,
SIMPSON,
W. F. IRWIN,

Drs. J. S. IRWIN,
BURRELL,
ARMSTRONG,
M'CONNELL,
SPEER,
DENNY,
HANNEN,
M'FARLANE;

Houses of Worship.

The Roman Catholic church, is situated at the upper end of Liberty street.—Pastor, Rev. CHARLES B. MAGUIRE.

The Protestant Episcopal church is situated on the south side of 6th, between Wood and Smithfield streets. Pastor, Rev. JOHN H. HOPKINS.

Of this building, we present our readers with a sketch from the pencil of the reverend gentlemen just mentioned, and from the graver of Mr. William Savory, of our city. The structure is in the Gothic style, and was designed by Mr. Hopkins, who has, in its plan and construction exhibited his usual superior knowledge, and a most discrim-

9

inating taste. We have not room to enter into a detail of the architecture, or the economy of the edifice. The interior, however, with one exception, is perfectly consonant with the exterior. Our exception is to the ceiling, which, instead of being vaulted, is entirely flat, presenting a considerable contrast to the heavily arched windows, the springing arches between the columns, and the deep and vaulted recess of the pulpit. The defect, is in some measure relieved by ornamental wood-work running transversely from opposite columns. Taking it all together, it is a majectic pile, and there are few who will refuse it the merit of being among the handsomest churches in our country.

The first Presbyterian church, E. side of Wood street, between Virgin alley and 6th street.—Pastor, Rev. Francis Herron.

The Second Presbyterian church, North west corner of Smithfield street and Diamond alley.—Pastor, Rev. E. P. Swift.

Seceder's, corner of Seventh street and Cherry alley.—Pastor, Rev. Robert Bruce.

Covenanter's, S. side of Plumb alley, between Liberty and Cherry alley.—Pastor, Rev. John Black.

First Methodist church, N. side of Front, between Wood and Smithfield streets.

Second Methodist church, S. E. corner of Smithfield and Seventh streets.—Present Pastor, Rev. —— Stevens.

German Lutheran, N. E. corner of Smithfield and 6th streets.

Associate Reformed, N. W. corner of 6th street and Cherry alley Pastor, Rev. Joseph Kerr.

Baptist, N. E. corner of 3d and Grant streets.

Unitarian, E. side of Smithfield, between Sixth street and Virgin alley.—Pastor, Rev.——Swartzwelder.

Education.

There are in Pittsburgh, upwards of forty academies, schools, and other places of learning. Among the most prominent of these, is the Western University of Pennsylvania. The liberal patronage of the late Legislature, towards it, we trust, will secure to the institution, that respectability and standing which the talents of its professors ought to command.

The following gentlemen are the professors:

Rev. R. Bruce, Principal, and Professor of Natural Philosophy &c.
Rev. J. Black, Professor of Ancient Languages and Classical Literature.
Rev. E. P. Swift, Professor of Moral Sciences.
Rev. C. B. Maguire, Professor of Modern Languages.
Rev. J. H. Hopkins, Professor of Rhetoric and Belles-Lettres.

The new University buildings will be commenced this year.

DIRECTORY

OF THE

CITY OF PITTSBURGH,

FOR THE YEAR

Eighteen Hundred and Twenty=six.

ALPHABETICAL LIST

OF THE STREETS, LANES. ALLEYS, COURTS, &c.

IN THE CITY.

EIGHTH street, running from the upper end of Liberty, parallel with the Monongahela.

Ferry street, from the Monongahela to 4th street, next below Chancery lane.

Fifth street, parallel with the Monongahela.

Fourth do. do. do. do.

Front do. do. do. do.

Grant st. from the Monongahela to Liberty, next above Smithfield.

Hand street, from Liberty to the Allegheny, next above Irwin.

Hay do. from Liberty to the Allegheny, next above Pitt.

High do. on Grant's hill, running from coal lane to Watson's road.

Irwin do. from Liberty to the Allegheny, next above St. Clair.

Liberty do. from the Monongahela, parallel with the Allegheny to the city line.

Marbury street, from Liberty to the Allegheny, nearly opposite the mouth of Third.

Market street, from the Monongahela to Liberty, passing the court house.

Penn street, from the Monongahela, parallel with, and next to the Allegheny.

Pitt street, from Liberty to the Allegheny, next below St. Clair.

Ross do. from the Monongahela to 4th, next above Grant.

Second street, parallel with the Monongahela.

Seventh do. do. do.

Sixth do. do. do.

Short do. from Monongahela to Liberty, next below Ferry.

Smithfield street, from the Monongahela bridge to Liberty, next
    above Wood.
St. Clair street, from Liberty to the Allegheny bridge.
Third street, parallel with the Monongahela river,
Try   do.   from the Monongahela to Fourth, next above Ross.
Union do.   N. W. corner of the Diamond to 5th.
Washington street, N. E. boundary, from Liberty to the Allegheny.
Water street, on the bank of the Monongahela.
Wayne st. from Liberty to the Allegheny, next below Washington.
West street, from the Monongahela to Liberty, next above Short.
Wood do.   from the Monongahela river to Liberty.

LANES.

Chancery lane, running from the Monongahela to 4th, between
    Market and Ferry.
Coal lane, from Grant street on top of Grant's hill, to coal pits.

ALLEYS.

Academy alley, running from Smithfield to Cherry alley, between
    2d and 3d streets.
Adams' alley, from Penn to the Allegheny, between Irwin st. and
    Barker's alley.
Brewery alley, from Marbury to the Monongahela, between Penn
    and Liberty.
Bell's alley, from Liberty to Penn, bet. Marbury & Monongahela.
Bakewell's alley, from Water to Front, between Cherry alley and
    Grant street.
Barker's alley, from Liberty street to Allegheny, next below Irwin.
Bowen's alley, from Penn   do.   do.   between Pitt st.
    and Cecil's alley.
Cecil's alley, from Liberty to the Allegheny, next below St. Clair.
Carpenter's alley, from 6th street to Virgin alley, west of Smithfield.
Cherry alley, from Monongahela to Liberty, between Smithfield and
    Grant streets.
Church alley, from 6th st. to Strawberry alley, east of Wood.
Diamond alley, from Liberty to Grant through the centre of Public
    Square.
Fayette alley, from Hand street to Garrison alley, between Penn and
    Cherry.
Foster's alley, from 6th to Strawberry alley, next above Cherry.
Garrison alley, from Liberty to the Allegheny, next above Hand st.
Harris' alley, from Virgin alley to 5th st. between Wood & Smithfield.
Hillsborough alley, from Virgin alley to 5th street, west of Wood.
Hay-scale alley, from 3d to 4th streets, west of Wood.
Irwin's alley, from Liberty to the Allegheny, next below Hand street.
Jackman's alley, from Irwin street to Adams' alley, west of Penn.
Jail alley, from 4th to Liberty, next west of Market
King's alley, from 5th to Virgin alley, east of Market.
Miltenberger's alley, from Strawberry alley to 7th st. east of Smithfield
Madison alley, from Hand st to Garrison alley, between Penn & Liberty
Maddock's alley, from Penn to the Allegheny, next above Irwin st.

M'Cormick's alley, from Penn to the Allegheny, next below Hand st.
Plumb alley, from Liberty to Grant street, between 7th & 8th streets.
Petticoat alley, from Miltenberger's alley to Smithfield.
Redoubt alley, from Monongahela to Liberty, next below Ferry st.
Stevenson's alley, from Liberty to the Allegheny, next below Hay.
Strawberry alley, from Liberty to Grant, next above mouth of Wood.
Union alley, from 6th to Strawberry alley, between Smithfield and
    Cherry alley.
Virgin alley, from Liberty to Grant, next above the mouth of Market.

COURTS.

Bakewell's Court, W. side of Water, between Grant and Ross streets.
Killemoon's   '   S. side of Virgin alley, between Wood & Smithfield.
Miltenberger's Court, N. side of Front, between Market and Ferry.
M'Clurg's Court, W. side of Smithfield, between Virgin alley & 5th st.
M'Masters'   '   N. side of Diamond alley, between W. & Smithfield.
Roseburg's   '   N. side of 5th, above Wood street.
Richmond's   '   N. side of 5th, between Wood and Smithfield.
Stewart's   '   S. side of 5th, between Wood and Smithfield.
Toman's   '   S. side of Virgin alley, between Wood & Smithfield.

ROWS.

Bayard's Row, north east corner of Liberty and sixth streets.
Gray's Row, running from the corner of Penn and St. Clair, to the
    Allegheny bridge.

—◦◦◦◦—

REMARKS.

APPLICATION was made, some months since, to the city Councils,
for the passage of an ordinance, authorising the *numbering* of the houses, and the designation of the streets and alleys, by *index boards*. As
these were improvements much desired by the citizens, generally, little doubt was entertained of their meeting the approbation of the corporate legislature. A committee was, indeed, appointed, to examine
and inquire &c.—but since then, we have heard nothing of the matter. The gentlemen selected, thought the subject, either unworthy
of their *legislative* consideration, or that the attention demanded by
their private concerns could not be sacrificed for a moment to public
benefit. We cannot see the propriety of electing men into office, or
of men accepting stations, to the duties of which, they do not, and will
not attend, although bound so to do, as well by their election, as by a
solemn obligation. It is with the greatest difficulty, sometimes, that
a quorum of our Councils can be brought together; and very often, on
days of meeting no business whatever is done, owing to non-atten-
dance. We must admit, that on election occasions, there is an unusual bustle and stir among our city senators and representatives; a
very notable requirement of clean shirts, sunday clothes, and all that
sort of thing; a look of becoming importance too, is manifestly visible
in the physiognomy of every one, that bespeaks the great events
which may call forth their wisdom and power in *futuro*. But, when

9*

all is over, and friends are served, the council-man returns to his domicil; resumes his apron; buries himself in the business of his avocation,
and there entirely forgets that he is one of the dignitaries of the corporation. For this apathy, only one, and a most cogent reason, may be
advanced—that is, there is no salary; no compensation attached to the
office—and as to the honour derived from it, as honest Jack Falstaff
says, "it will not set a leg, nor an arm; no," nor even set an "*esq.*"
to the hinder end one's cognomen.   Now, we would beg leave to
hazard an assertion, and feel no objection to risque our reputation on
the issue, that if the members of the Councils, were each to receive
but one dollar per diem, for each and every day's attendance upon
their official duties, there would scarcely be an absent council-man on
any occasion; and there is not the smallest particle of doubt in our
minds that their meetings would be *less* numerous than heretofore.
Or if a pecuniary compensation could not be given, there would be a
mighty stimulus in another mode of rewarding their labours—we mean
an occasional good hot supper, such as are generally served up to the
corporate authorities of the east on days of city legislation.   There is
something in these feasts so enticing; the mind is anticipating the good
things many days before; the business to be done, is, consequently, often thought of, as being particularly indentified with the *finale.*—Every thing goes on so snug, that when the long expectant member sits
down to the "groaning board," he is forced to rub his hands together,
and exclaim with old Kit Cosey, in the play, "*Ah, this is what I call
comfortable!*"   Reward is the great lever of human action and enterprize, and almost every man thinks now-adays with Franklin, that
"time is money."—Therefore, our city councils require something at
our hands, to enable them to attend to their duties and to compensate
them for their time—something that will either drive *vacuity* out of
their *pockets; vacuity* out of their *heads,* or *vacuity* out of their *stomachs.*

————

☞ DIRECTIONS—the houses not being numbered, as before
intimated, we are compelled to designate them in the old way, to wit:
the four points, by initials, as N. S. E. W. n will stand for near ; c for
corner ; b for between; dw for dwelling; s for side, and sometimes, al
for alley. When 2d, 3d or 4th, or any such designations occur, they
are intended as 2d, 3d or 4th *streets.*

*As there are many names that are or may be spelled in different ways,
persons wishing to find one of this kind, will be pleased, if they fail in the
first instance, to persevere, and seek it under every initial that may present a probability of discovery.*

DIRECTORY,

SHEWING THE NAMES AND HABITATIONS OF EVERY
CITIZEN, &c. RESIDING IN

Pittsburgh, Allegheny Town, Kensington, Birmingham and N. Liberties.

A

ANSHUTZ GEORGE, Jr. gent. S side 2d b Smithfield and Cherry alley.
Algeo Thomas, gent. S side 5th near Smithfield.
Algeo John, grocer, N side Liberty, b Irwin st. & Irwin alley.
Armorer Joseph, merchant, E side Market, b Liberty & 5th.
Alexander Hugh, butcher, S side 5th b Wood and Market.
Adams James, cot. manufacturer, N W c of Irwin and Liberty
Abercrombie James, bricklayer, S side Diamond alley, b Wood and Smithfield.
Allison John, carter, Maddock's alley.
Ash Sarah, seamstress, N side Penn, near Bowen's alley.
Armstrong John, blacksmith, S side 2d near Liberty.
Albree John, shoe merchant, shop W side Market, near the Diamond; dwelling N side 4th b Wood and Smithfield.
Adams Gabriel, grocer, N side 1st near Market.
Alexander William, cabinet maker, S W corner of 2d and Market.
Agnew James, doctor, N W corner of Chancery lane and 2d.
Armstrong Charles L. doctor, W side of Market near Front.
Avery Charles, druggist, Penn, b Wayne and Washington.
Avery & Co. druggists, S E c of 2d and Wood.
  do.   do.   do.   N E c of 4th and Market.
Arthurs William, cotton spinner, S side of 7th b Cherry alley & Grant
Arthurs John, engineer, S side 7th near Cherry alley.
Anderson John, late constable, Union alley, b 6th and Cherry alley.
Adams Mary, widow, N side Front, b Ferry and Chancery lane.
Alexander Alexander, Sen. nailor, N side 5th b Wood and Smithfield.
Anshutz & Rahm, com. merchants, E side Wood b Front and Water.
Allen & Grant, com. merchants, S side of Front, b Wood and Market.
Allen Michael, com. merchant, N side Water, b Wood and Market.
Adams David, forgeman, E side High, n coal lane.
Allen Lewis, labourer, N side Diamond alley, n Smithfield.
Adams & Hutchison, com. merchants, S side Front, b Market & Wood.
Anderson William, auctioneer, store N E c of Wood and Front: dwelling S E c of 2d and Smithfield.
Andoe John, grocer, E side of Market, b the Diamond and 5th.
Anshutz Christian, com. merchant, E side of Wood b Front & Water.
Alexander Alexander, Jr. nailor, N side 5th b Wood & Smithfield.

Allison Andrew, labourer, N s 2d, b Market and Wood.
Abbot George & Co. shoemakers, W s Wood, b Front and 2d.
Arthurs William, at Arthurs' Factory.
Arthurs Robert, fuller do.   do.
Arthurs James, Jr. engineer, do.
Adams James, jr. clerk at S. A. Dubarry's store.
Armstrong James, grocer, N s Diamond alley, b Wood and Market.
Anderson Hugh, clerk at Anderson's auction store.
Ayres James, carpenter, N s Front, b Short and Redoubt alley.
Armstrong Andrew, weaver, Northern Liberties.
Anderson Robert, labourer   do
Artzt Charles, Machinist, Kensington.
Andrews John, Rev. Allegheny town.
Ackley Henry, butcher,   do
Allen Joseph,   do
Anderson James, brick-maker, do
Andrews & Waugh, editors of the Statesman, Office S side 4th b
     Market and Chancery lane.
Andrews John C. printer, dwelling N side 3d, b Wood and Smithfield.
Agen Stephen, wagon maker, at Lecky's.
Allen Lewis, tobacconist, N side Diamond alley, b Wood & Smithfield.
Alexander & Beatty, stone cutters, Liberty, E of the Chapel.
Armstrong James, inkeeper, S side Penn, b St. Clair and Cecil's alley.
Allender Joseph, carter, S side of Penn, b St. Clair and Cecil's alley.
Allender Rebecca, milliner   do.   do.   do.
Algeo Wm. clerk, at O'Hara's glass works.
Andrews John, editor of Recorder, S side 4th b Ferry & Chancery l.
Alexander Francis, blacksmith, W side of Liberty n 6th.
Abercrombie Elizabeth, milliner shop, S side of Diamond alley.
     b Wood and Smithfield.
Atchenson Moses, S side Strawberry alley, b Wood and Smithfield.
Anderson Wm. shoemaker, S side 5th, b Wood and Smithfield.
Adams Archibald, blacksmith,   do.   do.
Arthurs Thomas, labourer, M'Cormick's alley.
Alexander Samuel, stone cutter, N side Penn, b Hand & Irwin's alley.
Argo James, carpenter, W side Smithfield, b Strawberry alley & 7th.
Aikens James, labourer,   do.   do.   do.   do.
Algeo Rebecca, widow, S. side Liberty, b Smithfield and 7th.
Applegate —— widow, seamstress, Bakewell's court.
Adams Benjamin, glass cutter, N side Front, b Grant and Ross.
Arthurs Thomas, labourer,   do   do.   do.
Anderson John, gent. S side 2d   do.
Annis Levi B. blacksmith, S side 3d, b Grant and Ross.
Addis Isaac, carpenter, E side High st.
Anderson Biddy, laundress, N side Front, between Smithfield and
     Cherry alley.
Allen Robert, labourer, N. side 3d, b Wood and Smithfield.
Anderson John, labourer, E side Miltenberger's alley.
Armstrong Elizabeth, widow, E side Smithfield, b 6th and Virgin al.
Anderson Thomas, labourer, E side Cherry alley, b 6th and Straw-
     berry alley.
Anderson Wm. shoemaker, S side Strawberry alley, b Cherry alley
     and Smithfield.

Ashly John, book-binder, E side Carpenter's alley.
Algeo Gregg, merchant, W side   do.
Anderson John W. clerk at Anderson's auction store.
Anderson John, carpenter, N s Virgin alley, b Smithfield & Cherry al.
Abrahams James, carpenter, Killemoon's court, Virgin alley.
Ashby Charles, tailor, S s 5th, b Wood and Market.
Anderson Wm. grocer, E s Wood, b Virgin alley and 5th.
Abrahams Joseph, currier, S s Diamond alley, b Jail alley & Liberty:
Addington David, tobacconist, W s Jail alley, next the Jail.
Applegate Andrew, carpenter, N s 4th, b Jail alley and Liberty.
Alexander Sarah & Rachel, milliners and bonnet makers, S s 4th, b
    Ferry and Chancery lane.
Ashly Charles, tailor, N E c Market and 2d.
Andrews Agnes, widow, spooler, E s Ferry, b Front and 2d.
Amberson Silas, labourer, S s 2d, b Market and Chancery lane.

B

Bell John, grocer, W s Liberty, c of Bell's alley.
Bell Mary, widow, E s Penn, c of Bell's alley.
Berry Wm. boat-builder, brewery alley, n the river.
Bushnell Alexander, blockmaker, S s Penn, n Marbury.
Boyd David, ship carpenter, W s Marbury, b Penn and Brewery al.
Bell Robert, blacksmith, S s 2d, n Liberty.
Brown George W. boat builder, bank of the river, n Liberty.
Brackenridge Alexander, attorney, N E c of Penn and Marbury.
Bryson Samuel, inkeeper, W s Grant, b 2d and 3d.
Bruce Robert, Rev. S W c of 2d and Cherry alley.
Brown Allen, tanner, S W c of Front and Cherry alley.
Blair Wm. brushmaker and county treasurer, E s Wood, b 5th and
    Virgin alley.
Byrne John, dyer & umbrella maker, N s 3d, b Market and Wood.
Barclay Joseph, gauger, No. 6, Gray's row, St. Clair.
Burrill Thomas, doctor, S s 3d, b Market and Wood.
Barker Abner, gent. N s Penn, n St. Clair.
Beard Peter, baker and confectioner, W s Wood, b 3d and 4th.
Burgess John, merchant, store S E c of Market and 4th, dw N s Lib-
    erty, c of Stevenson's alley.
Baily Francis, distiller, N s Front, b Wood and Market.
Brunot Felix, doctor, S s Liberty, n Virgin alley.
Bakewell Benjamin, glass manufacturer, N W c of 4th and Grant.
Brown James, baker and merchant, store W s Market, n 5th, dw.
    in Allegheny town.
Brewer Charles, merchant, store N s 5th n Market, dw N W c of
    Liberty and Cecil's alley.
Baldwin Henry, Esq. attorney, at John Davis', Water st.
Biddle Richard, Esq. attorney, S s 4th, b Wood and Market.
Biddle Samuel, barber, S s Liberty, b Strawberry alley and 7th, n
    Beitler's tavern.
Beitler John, inkeeper, S s Liberty, b Strawberry alley & Smithfield.
Burt William, paver and grocer, No. 8 Gray's Row.

Baum Wm. P. tinner, N E c of Wood and 2d, also toy shop, E s
Wood, b 2d and 3d.

Bartram James A. clerk, Water, n Ferry.

Baily Robert, grocer, S E c of the Diamond.

Boss Daniel C. inkeeper, Water, b Ferry and Chancery lane.

Bowers Fidele, dairy-man, N s 7th, n Grant.

Burke Robert, attorney, office and dw. in the Diamond, b Diamond
alley and Union st

Beal George, inkeeper, brush and bellows manufacturer, W s Diamond
c of Diamond alley.

Beelen Anthony, merchant, S s of Front, b Market and Wood, dw.
in Water, b Market and Wood.

Balsly Benjamin, mason or laborer, S s Virgin alley, n Liberty.

Baily Francis & Co. merchants, N s Liberty, b Hand and Irwin's alley

Baily Francis, merchant, S s Penn, b Hand and Irwin's alley.

Baxter Henry, blacksmith, N E c of 5th and Hillsborough alley.

Baker Jacob, blacksmith, N W c of Grant and 2d.

Baily Wm. glass cutter, S s 2d, b Cherry alley and Smithfield.

Byrne Franklin S. portrait, sign and ornamental painter and gilder, N
s 2d, b Wood and Market, opposite the Post office.

Bell William, jr. merchant, store S W c of Wood and 3d.

Baggs Andrew, painter, S W c of Front and Smithfield.

Bowen Richard, N s of Penn, b Pitt and Stevenson's alley.

Black David, wagoner, N s Diamond alley, at Hugh M'Masters'.

Blasdell Aaron, merchant, N W c of Diamond and Market.

Baker Sandy, chair-maker, and ornamental painter, N s of 4th b Market and Jail alley.

Boggs & Wrenshall, merchants, S W c of 4th and Market.

Boggs George, merchant, dw S E c of Grant and 2d.

Baird Samuel, merchant, W s Market, b 4th and the Diamond, dw N
s 4th, b Wood and Market.

Baker Adam, tobacconist, S s 5th, b Wood and Smithfield.

Breed George, merchant, W s Market, b 5th and Diamond, dw S s 4th,
b Wood and Market.

Black Joseph, clerk at Stewart's Hotel.

Bevan Richard, grocer, E s Wood, b 2d and 3d.

Blair David, shop keeper, S s Liberty, b Virgin al and 6th.

Barker Henry, mate steam boat, at Boss' tavern.

Barcly Andrew, horse auctioneer, W s St. Clair, b Penn and Liberty.

Bringhurst William, coach painter, at Lecky's.

Burns Bernard, grocer, E s Wood, b Liberty and 6th.

Brown Samuel, labourer, S E c of 4th and Smithfield.

Bayard Ross, clerk, N s Front, b Ferry and Chancery lane.

Bradly Patrick, tailor, S W c Wood and Front.

Brawdy Aaron, grocer, W s Wood, b Front & Water.

Boreland Moses, painter, N s 2d, b Grant and Cherry alley.

Burt Nancy, widow, carpet weaver, N side 4th, b market & Jail alley
one loom.

Brown Sarah, tailoress, W s Market, b the Diamond and 4th.

Baker John, paper maker, in paper mill yard.

Baker Margaret, widow,   do   do   do

Bradly Richard, nailor, Bowen's alley.

Bradly Charles, carpenter,   do

Brickle George, engineer, Bowen's alley.

Birmingham Jane, widow, seamstress, Bowen's alley.

Bradly George W. tailor, shop E s Market, b 2d and Front, dw N s 2d b Cherry alley and Grant.

Bissel John, merchant, S s Penn, b Pitt & Cecils al.

Barr John, carter, N s Diamond al. b Wood and Smithfield.

Beltzhoover Mary, boarding house, N s Diamond alley, b Wood and Smithfield.

Brown William, carter, Stewart's court, 5th st.

Baird David, labourer, S s 5th, b Wood and Smithfield.

Belvail Catharine, tailoress, S s 5th, b Wood and Smithfield.

Brown James H. cooper, shop N s 5th, b Wood and do dw S s 5th. b Wood and Smithfield

Boyd Samuel, tobacconist, N s Liberty, b Irwin's street & Irwin's al.

Beeler Samuel, shoemaker, W s Wood, b 5th and Diamond al.

Brokew Bergin, shoemaker, W s Wood, b Front & Water.

Borbidge & Cunningham, carpenters, S W c of Diamond al & Smithf.

Borbidge James, grocer, No. 11 Gray's Row.

Bigham Samuel, labourer, S s Penn, b Irwin and Barker's alley.

Bean John, carpenter, at Kerr's tavern, Diamond.

Bradly Isabella, widow, W s Irwin, b Penn and Allegheny.

Brown John, blacksmith, Maddock's alley.

Beatty William, do   do

Beatty Eli, turner,   do

Boswell George, weaver, N s Penn, b Irwin and Maddock's al.

Bradford Thomas, grocer, N side Penn, b Hand and Irwin's al.

Britt Edward, labourer, Irwin's alley, near the Allegheny.

Barr Samuel, weaver, c of Plumb al and Liberty.

Bowers John, shoemaker, S s Strawberry al b Liberty & Smithfield.

Balsly Michael, tobacconist, W s Smithfield, b 7th & Strawberry al.

Barnes Samuel, gent. N s Liberty, b Hand and Garrison alley.

Brewerton Job, coffee-mill maker, shop N E c of 7th and Smithfield dw S s 2d, b Grant and Ross.

Beans John, carpenter, N s 7th, b Cherry al and Smithfield.

Burton Thomas, jr. shoemaker, S s 7th b Cherry al do

Barnes David, boarding house, E s of Grant, b Front & Water.

Barefoot James, labourer, Carpenter's alley.

Burnsides Robert, wheelwright, shop N E c of 5th and Smithfield dw S s Front, b Grant and Ross.

Berryhill William, shoemaker, N s Front, b Grant and Ross.

Brickle James, cabinet maker, N s 2d   do   do

Bracken William, bricklayer, N s 2d   do   do

Brown James, drayman, N s 2d   do   do

Bratt James, pudler, N s 2d   do   do

Burton William, shoemaker, N s   do   do

Bishop Joseph, drayman, N s 2d   do   do

Brown Tristram, boarding house, S s Liberty, b Diamond al and 4th.

Boocher John, blacksmith, S s 3d, b Grant and Ross.

Boocher Eve, nurse, S s   do   do

Boocher William, shoemaker,   do   do

Barford Peter, laborer, S s   do   do

Barcly Ann, widow, laundress,   do   do

Borbidge Joseph, carpenter, E s High street.

Barndoller David, laborer, E s Ross, b 3d and 4th.
Brown James, weaver, N s 3d, b Grant and Ross.
Brown John, gent. S s 2d, b Grant and Cherry alley.
Barnhill William, blacksmith, N s Water, b Cherry al and Smithfield.
Brady Elizabeth, shoebinder, Bakewell's alley.
Bulford Simeon, chair maker, S s Front, b Cherry alley and Grant.
Black Martha, widow, S s Front   do   do
Bulford Ann, widow, milliner, S E c of 3d and Cherry al.
Binny James. engineer, N s Front, b Wood and Smithfield.
Boner Charles, waiter, N s 3d   do   do
Butler Martha, widow, boarding house, N s 3d, b Wood & Smithfield.
Beal & Konecke, merchants, No. 2 Bayard's Row.
Blair David, carpenter, N s Liberty, b Irwin's st. and Irwin's alley.
Baggs Sarah, widow, N s Diamond al b Wood and Smithfield.
Becum Mary, widow, seamstress, N s Miltenberger's alley.
Burns James, labourer, Petticoat alley.
Bradshaw George, grocer, E s Smithfield, b Virgin al and 6th.
Barr William, drayman, S E c of Smithfield and 6th.
Benson Charles, labourer, N s Strawberry b Cherry & Miltenberger's al
Berry William, ship carpenter, N s   do   do
Boyd Joseph, labourer, S s 7th b Cherry al and Grant.
Black James. mate of steam boat, W s Smithfield, b Virgin al & 6th.
Barnet David, carpenter, S s 6th, b Cherry alley and Smithfield.
Barr Nancy, widow, spinner, S s do   do
Barnet Thomas, carpenter, S s   do   do
Baird Elizabeth, widow, S s Virgin alley, b Wood and Smithfield.
Brown Samuel, water hauler, S s do   do   do
Barnes George, N s 5th, b Wood and Smithfield.
Barker Wm. blacksmith, N s do   do
Barnwell John, tailor, E s Jail al n Liberty.
Brewer Philo, shoemaker, W side Jail al next the Jail.
Brook Susan, widow, laundress, W s Jail al do
Barber John, doctor, office S E c of the Diamond.
Brooks James, nailor, S E c of 5th and Liberty.
Byrnes Charles, tailor, N E c of Liberty and Virgin alley.
Blair David, grocer, S s Liberty, b Virgin al and 6th.
Burroff Henry, shoemaker, W s King's al.
Brown Peter, labourer,   do   do
Bell Thomas, blacksmith,   do   do
Barr John, shoemaker, E s Market, b 2d and 3d
Black and Marlatt, shoemakers, E s Market, b 2 and 3d.
Banton John, ship carpenter, S E c of Ferry and 2d.
Baird John D. & Co. com. merchants, N s of Water, b Ferry and
     Chancery Jane.
Baird Thomas, clerk, N E c of Ferry and Front.
Banton William, tinner, Miltenberger's court, Front st.
Baggs William, engineer, S s 2d, b Ferry and Redoubt alley.
Bracken Mary, widow, boarding house, W s Market, b 3d and 4th.
Beer Thomas, freighter, S s 3d, b Wood and Market.
Barnwell Eleanor, boarding house, S s 3d, b Market & Wood.
Black Martha, widow, tailoress, N s 3d,   do   do
Burk William, labourer, E s Hillsborough alley.
Beatty John, stone cutter, W s Liberty, b Virgin alley and 6th.

Butler James R. military store-keeper, U. S. Arsenal.
Brady Patrick, tailor, S W c of Wood and Front.
Bakewell Thomas, glass manufacturer, at glass house.
Bank of Pittsburgh, S W c of Market and 3d.
Bank of U. S. 2d, b Chancery lane and Ferry.
Black George, shop keeper, Allegheny town
Boyd John, carpenter   do
Barr James, brickmaker   do
Brown James, baker   do
Butler Jerusha, widow   do
Bowman Robert, carpenter   do
Barlow Thomas, gent.   do
Bennett William, tanner   do
Boyle Alexander, pilot   do
Brooksham Joseph, forgeman, Kensington.
Brickle John, engineer   do
Bryant George, engineer   do
Burns Andrew, shoemaker   do
Boyd William, drayman   do
Brooks Howard, carter   do
Brunot Hilary, white lead manufacturer, Northern Liberties.
Burns Arthur, labourer   do
Brown James, quarry-man   do
Bell John, labourer   do
Bayard John, tanner   do
Bayard George, gent.   do
Barclay James, grocer   do
Becom John, labourer   do
Bagley Josiah, carpenter   do
Brown Michael, gent.   do
Baldridge Elias, brewer   do
Burgess Francis, woollen weaver   do
Bratt Moses, refiner   do
Bynon David, pudler   do
Bynon Edward   do   do
Baggs David, carpenter   do
Brown Peter, laborer   do
Bickerton Mary, teacher   do
Bell Richard, labourer   do
Bausman Rhinehart A. constable, Birmingham.
Barr James, potter   do
Brickle George, farmer   do
Brooks Mary, widow   do
Bausman William, coal digger   do
Burns Henry, ferryman   do
Bryan James, broom maker   do
Biglow Elijah, labourer   do
Bryan Samuel, refiner   do
Brier John, labourer   do

10

C

CHAMBERS CHARLES, labourer, S s Penn, n Marbury.
Calvert James, labourer,   do   do   do
Caldwell John, tanner, N s 2d b Ferry st and Redoubt alley.
Church William, doctor, S s 4th b Wood and Smithfield.
Coyle Bernard, jailor, Jail alley n 4th.
Cooper James, clerk of the market, W s Penn, below Wayne.
Cramer & Spear, printers and booksellers, E s Wood b 3d and 4th.
Closey Webb, boot and shoemaker, W s Market, b Front and 2d, dw
    N s Front, b Ferry st and Chancery lane.
Christy Robert, alderman, office N E c of the Diamond and Union st.
    dw N s 3d b Ferry st and Chancery lane.
Carson John, pump maker S s 2d b Cherry alley and Grant sts.
Camblin William, labourer, S s 4th b Wood and Smithfield.
Crail Thomas, carpenter, S s Virgin alley, b Wood and Smithfield.
Cargill James, board merchant, N s Irwin, b Penn and the Allegheny.
Caldwell Margaret, shop-keeper, W s Wood b Virgin alley and 5th st.
Croxford William, glass-cutter, N s 3d b Grant and Ross.
Cooper Thomas, alderman N s Front n Smithfield.
Craft James S. attorney at law, N E c of Water st and Chancery lane,
    office S E c of Front st and Chancery lane.
Cullen Moses, gent. N W c Diamond and Diamond alley.
Crawford Wm. cabinet maker and street com. N s 4th b Wood and
    Market.
Callan James, teacher, N s 5th b Market and Wood.
Cotter Florence, wharf-master, N E c of Front and Ferry.
Chambers John, shoemaker, N side Liberty opposite Wood.
Cairns William, shoemaker, N s Diamond alley b Wood and Smithf.
Cheetham Algernon S. grocer, E s Market n Water.
Carlisle Nathan, grocer, No. 2 Gray's Row.
Carron J. Louis V. barber, E s Wood b 2d and 3d.
Correy James, cashier br. B. U. S. at banking house, 2d above Ferry.
Connelly & Gay, merchants, S E c of Front and Wood.
Carson James, toll receiver, Allegheny bridge.
Cuthbert Sturley, iron-founder, N s 5th b Smithfield and Wood.
Cooper William L. blacksmith, S s Virgin alley above Wood st.
Collingwood Thomas, paver, Virgin alley, b Wood and Liberty.
Curtis Elliott, carpenter, No. 3 Gray's Row.
Conner Cornelius, clerk, N E c of Ferry and Front.
Crossan James, innkeeper, N E c of Wood and 4th.
Cole Rufus, grocer, S E c of the Diamond.
Cummins James C. S E c of Liberty st and Virgin alley.
Cecil Miss Susan, store-keeper, W s Liberty st. n Cecil's alley.
Craig Charles, grocer and overseer of poor, S W c of Wood st and
    Diamond alley.
Christy John, bell-ringer, S s 4th b Market and Wood.
Clingan Thomas, tinner, S s 3d b Wood and Market.
Cuddy James, iron-founder, N s 5th b Wood and Smithfield.
Crane George, shoemaker, N s Front b do   do
Clendennin Levi, paper-maker, paper mill yard.
Conologue Owen, labourer, E s Pitt n the Allegheny.

Craig Thomas, nailor, Bowen's alley.
Carey John, freighter, S s 7th b Cherry alley and Grant st.
Curry John, roller, *W* s Penn b Pitt st and Cecil's alley.
Claridge Loyd, chairmaker, N s 4th b Wood and Smithfield.
Connelly James, labourer, N s Diamond al. b Wood and Smithfield.
Crawford Robert, tailor. S s   do   do   do
Carr Thomas, hatter, 4th st c of Hay-scale alley.
Carpenter George W. shoemaker, S s 4th b Wood and Market.
Childs Harvey, shoemaker, *W* s Wood, b 3d and 4th.
Charlton Joseph, grocer, N E c of Wood and 6th.
Charlton Thomas, weaver, do   do   do
Clare James, shoemaker, shop E s Wood b 5th and Virgin alley, dw
    Allegheny town.
Crawford Mary, widow, S s 5th b Wood and Smithfield.
Cochran George, silversmith, *W* s Wood b 5th st and Diamond alley.
Craig Neville B. attorney at law, office, S s Diamond, *W* of Market—
    dw 5th st N c of King's alley.
Coulter John, grocer, No. 4 Gray's Row.
Carrel Robert, ostler, Adam's alley.
Cochran Elizabeth, laundress, Adam's alley.
Crumley William, carter, Jackman's alley.
Camp Samuel, carter, *W* s Irwin b Penn and the Allegheny.
Crook John, trader, S E c of Irwin st and the Allegheny.
Conden John, labourer, E s Irwin, b Penn and the Allegheny.
Clark Lawrence, wagon-maker, do   do   do
Crowel Ephraim, brushmaker, Maddock's alley.
Cochran Samuel, innkeeper, N s Penn b Hand st and Irwin's alley.
Callaghan Jeremiah, labourer, M'Cormick's alley.
Connin Patrick   do   do
Calhoun Charles,   do   do
Chambers John, carpenter, N s Penn b Garrison alley and Wayne st.
Crowley Jeremiah, carpenter, S s Strawberry alley b Liberty and
    Smithfield.
Coyle James, carpenter,   do   do   do
Conn John, shoemaker,   do   do   do
Carson Robert, cooper,   do   do   do
Carson William, cooper, N s 6th below Smithfield.
Cannon Samuel, carpenter, N s 7th b Smithfield st and Cherry alley.
Clow James, clerk, S s 7th b   do   do
Carrel Daniel, teazer, N side Water b Grant and Ross.
Cameron Nancy, widow, do   do   do   do
Cole Susanna, widow,   do   do   do   do
Carrol James, cabinet maker, S s 2d b Grant and Ross.
Coates James, refiner, N s   do b   do   do
Carline Jacob, pudler, do   do   do   do
Coulter Joseph, mason, do   do   do   do
Chambers *W*illam, labourer, E s Grant, b 2d and 3d.
Cunningham Thomas, fisherman, S. *W.* c of 3d and Grant.
Cunningham James, carpenter, *W* s Ross b 2d and 3d.
Clark George, blacksmith, High street.
Childs *W*illiam, fireman, E s Ross b 3d and 4th.
Campbell John, glass-blower, N s 3d b Grant and Ross.
Cavin *W*illiam, lumber merchant, *W*ater, above Smithfield,

Carpenter James, book-binder, at Johnston and Stockton's.
Cooper Martin, boarding house, S s 2d just above Smithfield.
Campbell Joseph, carter, W s Smithfield b Virgin alley and 6th st.
Creighton James, blacksmith, do   do   do
Chambers James, carpenter, S 6th s b Smithfield st and Cherry alley.
Carr Samuel, bricklayer, E end of Virgin alley.
Croust Henry, blacksmith, Richmond's court.
Cashdoller Jacob, baker, S W corner of Kings and Virgin al.
Coxe Thomas, weaver, Hillsborough alley.
Conway Arthur, labourer, S s Diamond al n Liberty st.
Clark Samuel, ship-carpenter, next the jail, Jail alley.
Coolman C. attorney at law, N s Diamond n Union st.
Chambers Sarah, laundress, S s Liberty b Virgin al and 6th st.
Connelly Hugh, labourer, do   do   do   do
Cozens Jane, laundress, Kings alley.
Chapman Joel, carpenter, do   do
Caskey Joseph, grocer, N E c of 5th and Kings alley.
Coffin Abel, ship-carpenter, W s Ferry b 2d and 3d.
Curran Wm. carpenter, E s Ferry b Front and Water.
Craig Elizabeth, widow, S W c of Chancery lane and Front st.
Carrel Patrick, labourer, S s Front, b Market st and Chancery l.
Cary Isaac, cabinet-maker, &c. Front b Wood and Market.
Cuthbertson Mary, widow, N s do b do   do
Clayton Elijah, taylor, E s Marbury b Penn and Liberty.
Coulter Charles, weaver, N s Liberty b Hay and Marbury.
Clark Thomas, plane-maker, E s Penn below Irwin's alley.
Combs Joseph, blacksmith, Bakewell's alley.
Carr James, carpenter, S s 3d b Cherry alley and Grant st.
Carnahan Elizabeth, seamstress, E s Cherry alley, b Front and 2d.
Church Samuel, grocer,   do   do   do
Christy Samuel, constable, c of Academy and Cherry alleys.
Childs Asa, shoemaker, S W c of 2d and Smithfield.
Campbell John, teacher, N s 2d b Wood and Smithfield.
Cupples Joseph, drayman, E s Irwin b Penn and Liberty.
Corry James, labourer,   do do   do   do
Corry Charlotte, teacher, do do   do   do
Church Wm. hatter, E s Church alley.
Corr Jane, widow,   do
Cannon Thomas, chair-maker, N s 2d b Wood and Smithfield.
Campbell John, brick-maker, N s 6th b do   do
Craig Robert, drayman, Smithfield, b 6th st and Strawberry alley.
Catherwood John, labourer, Petticoat alley.
Carothers Nancy, tailoress,   do   do
Chapman Wm. weaver, E s Cherry al b 6th and Strawberry al.
Coyle John, blacksmith,   do   do   do
Carny John, labourer,   do   do   do
Clark James, weaver, S s Strawberry, b Cherry al and Grant.
Connelly Jesse, blacksmith, S s Strawberry b Cherry and Union al.
Curling Robert, clerk, Bakewell's glass house.
Cochran George, Agent of Domestic Manufac. Asso. dw N s 2d b
    Wood and Smithfield.
Crosby Joshua E. shoemaker, S side 2d b Ferry and Chancery lane.
Cunningham Wm. plasterer, S s 2d b Market and Wood.

Clark Miles, livery stable, N s 3d above Hay-scale alley.
Carr Edward, teacher,   do   below   do
Coyle Patrick, shopkeeper, N s 3d b Market and Wood.
Cassilly Thomas, innkeeper, Allegheny bridge.
Cassilly Peter, merchant, at Th. Cassilly's.
Cassilly Charles John, labourer, E s Smithfiield b Virgin alley and 6th.
Cassilly Charles & Peter, grocers, E s of Diamond, S of Diamond al.
Cutler William, shoemaker, N s Libery b Wayne st and Garrison al.
Caughey John, grocer, N s 3d b Wood and Smithfield.
Cosgreve Bartholomew, mason, N s Penn b Irwin st and Irwin's alley.
Collins Jane, gentlewoman, water st b Ferry st and Redoubt alley.
Chesnut Richard, wagoner, Birmingham.
Cairns Robert, coffee-mill-box maker, Birmingham.
Caldwell John, wagon maker,   do
Cunningham James, miller   do
Crilly Thomas, carpenter, Northern Liberties.
Cochran John, Esq.   do
Chaffee Harey, grocer   do
Cochran James, blacksmith   do
Curry James, nailor   do
Campbell Thomas, teacher   do
Colwell Thomas, nailor   do
Campbell Thomas, labourer, Kensington.
Coates John, pudler   do
Coates Ezekiel, pudler   do
Chambers James, labourer   do
Carr John, nailor   do
Cook Samuel, labourer   do
Campbell Robert, Inkeeper, Allegheny town.
Cameron John, brick-layer   do
Cook Walter, carpenter   do
Clark John,   do   do
Coyle John, boot and shoemaker,   do
Carothers Robert, weaver   do
Cupp Henry, carpenter   do
Capp Lodowick, shoemaker   do
Carson William, wagon maker   do
Conner John, mason   do
Cooney Patrick, labourer   do
Clare James G. boot and shoemaker, do.

D

DOUGHERTY JOHN, brick-maker, W s Liberty, n Bell's alley.
Dilworth John, ship-carpenter, E s Penn n Bell's alley.
Denny Harmar, attorney at law, c of Water and West.
Dobbins Mary, widow, S s 3d b Grant street and Cherry alley.
Duncan Jane, widow, E s Wood b Front and 2d
Deal Mary, widow, S s 2d, b Ferry and Chancery lane.
Davis William, gent. S W c of Kings and Virgin alleys.
Davis John, baker, shop E s Market b Front and 2d, dw in 2d b Market and Wood.

10 *

Dalzell John, grocer, store S E c of the Diamond and Diamond alley, dw N E c of Penn and Hay.

Drake Miss Jane, S s 5th b Wood and Market.

Doran Patrick, inn-keeper, W s of Diamond N of Diamond alley

Denny Wm. H. doctor, N s of 4th b Market and Wood.

Darlington Benjamin, hardware merchant, store, W s of Market b 3d and 4th, dw c of 3d and Chancery lane.

Davis John, gent. N E c of Water street and Redoubt alley.

Darragh John, esq. merchant, N W c of Market and 3d.

Dawson George, druggist, S E c of Wood and 4th

Davis & Hanson, auctioneers, N E c of Market and Front.

Davis John D. auct'r. dw   do   do

Denniston Samuel, innkeeper, N W c of Market and 2d.

Dickson Thomas, grocer, S s of Liberty, b Market st and Virgin alley.

Duncan Robert, shoemaker, S s 4th b Wood and Smithfield.

Douthitt John, boot & shoe maker, & ovs. of poor, Market b 3d & 4th.

Duff James, liquor merchant, N s of Diamond alley n the Diamond.

Diller William, tobacconist, N s of Liberty b. Hand st and Garrison al.

Davis Joseph, boarding-house, S s of 4th b Market and Ferry.

Dallas Trevanion B. attorney at law, office N s of 3d b Market st and Chancery lane, dw in Allegheny town n the bridge.

Dunlap Wm. carter, S s Diamond alley b Jail alley and Liberty.

Duncan Wm. D. com. merchant, warehouse S s Front b Market and Wood, dw N s of 3d b Ferry street and Chancery lane.

Develin Patrick, shoemaker, S s 3d b Grant and Ross

Duff William, grocer, N E c of Diamond alley and the Diamond.

Davis Thomas B. captain, Water 2 doors below Ferry.

Dennis Isaac, cooper, Barker's alley n the Allegheny.

Davenport James H. hatter, S side of Penn b St. Clair st and Cecil's al.

Donaldson William, Inkeeper, N s of Diamond alley, b the Diamond and Wood street.

Drake Andrew, grocer, S s of 6th b Wood and Liberty.

Darlington Samuel P. clerk, at Benjamin Darlington's.

Davis James H. merchant, E s of Diamond N of Diamond alley.

Daily William, clerk, at John Darragh's.

Duff Edward W. merchant, S s of Diamond alley b Market and Wood.

Dunlavy Jeremiah, inkeeper, S E c of 4th st and Redoubt alley.

Dimmit J. doctor, at Dr. Agnews.

Devinie John, barber and peruke maker, E s of Wood above 5th.

Dunlap Gon, carter, W s of Smithfield b 6th st and Virgin alley.

Dally & Co. grocers, E s of the Diamond, S of Diamond alley.

Dougherty George, pilot, N s of Water, b Ferry st. and Chancery l.

Dean Thomas, labourer, S s Penn b Pitt st. and Stevenson's alley.

Delver Edward, carter, N E corner of Penn and Pitt.

Douglass Robert, labourer, W s of Penn b Pitt st and Cecil's alley.

Dobbs George, labourer, N s Diamond alley, b Wood and Smithfield.

Douglass William, hatter, E side of Wood b Diamond alley and 4th st.

Dobbins James, Hatter, at Christopher Magee's

Darsie George, cabinet maker, N s 2d b Wood and Smithfield.

Dalzell James & Co. grocers, S E c of Liberty and Wood.

Dougherty Anthony, carter, S s of Liberty, next the Chapel.

Draer Jacob, bricklayer, S s of 5th b Wood and Smithfield,

Dougherty John, tailor, W s of Wood b 5th st and Virgin alley,

Drocourt Julius & Co. tinners, W s of Wood b Water and Front.
Develin Thomas, glass-cutter, S s of 3d b Grant and Ross
Dick Isabella, milliner, N s of Liberty, b St. Clair st and Cecil's alley.
Duffie Robert, labourer, Barker's alley n the Allegheny.
Donnelly Patrick, pedlar, Adams' alley.
Doyle Thomas, plasterer, N s of Irwin b Penn and the Allegheny.
Dillon James, pedlar,   do   do
Downing Dawson, shoemaker, do   do
Day Daniel, carpenter, Maddock's alley.
Donaldson Robert, turner, S s Penn b Hand st and Garrison alley.
Dewsnap Ellen, laundress, S s of Strawberry alley b Liberty and Smith.
Dalrymple Mary, widow, N s of Water b Grant and Ross.
Deary John, labourer, S s of Front b Grant and Ross.
Davis William, saddler, N side 2d b   do   do
Dalcleish John, labourer, E s Grant b 2d and 3d.
Devinie Elizabeth, widow, S s 3d b Grant and Ross.
Duval Jeremiah, carpenter, E s of High.
Davis Benjamin, blacksmith, do do
Davis Timothy, teacher, W s of Grant b Front and 2d.
Dryden George, glass cutter, S s of Front, b Grant st and Cherry alley.
Downer James C. innkeeper, Water above Wood.
Dodds Mary, widow, N s of 2d b Smithfield and Wood.
Delong Nancy, do S s of 3d b   do   do
Dewees Jesse, chair-maker, S s of 3d do   do
Davis John, bricklayer, E s Church alley.
Dixon Jane, widow, N s 6th b Church alley and Smithfield st.
Davidson Samuel, tobacconist, W s Smithfield b 6th st and Strawb. al.
Davidson Robert, segar-maker, N W c of 6th and Smithfield.
Downing John, carpenter, E s Miltenberger's alley.
Develin Thomas, carter, N E c of Strawberry and Miltenberger's al.
Douthit Jonathan, carter, E s Smithfield b 6th and Virgin alley.
Dimler John, labourer, S E c of Smithfield and 6th.
Dixon Wm. carpenter, W s Cherry al b 7th st and Strawberry alley.
Davidson James, tobacconist, W s Smithfield, b Virgin al and 7th st.
Dicky John, labourer, W s of Carpenter's alley.
Dickson John, coach and plough maker, Liberty above Virgin alley.
Dubarry S. A. & Co. merchants, W s Market b 3d and 4th.
Deary John, carpenter, E s Smithfield b Virgin alley and 5th st.
Dubois Joseph, carter, S s Virgin al b Wood and Smithfield.
Drake Joseph, fireman, N s 5th b   do   do
Davis Henry L. hatter, N s of 4th n Ferry.
Dickson Eliza, and sisters, milliners, S E c of 4th st and Chancery l.
Drennan David, clerk, Commissioner's office, dw E s Market b 5th
    and Liberty.
Donnelly Patrick, teacher, S s Liberty b Virgin alley and 6th st.
Davis Samuel, watch-maker, S s 5th b Wood and Market.
Dumars James, teacher, S s 3d b Wood and Smithfield.
Donnelly James, boat-builder, E s Ferry b Front and Water.
Dubois John, mate of s. b. Chancery lane b do   do
Drake Martha, tailoress,   do   do   do
Donnelly Patrick, labourer, S s of Front b Market st and Chancery l.
Drips William, tailor, S s 2d b Ferry st and Chancery lane.
Davis William, blacksmith do do   do

Davis William, cabinet maker, S s 2d b Market and Wood.
Dobbins Andrew, shoemaker, S s 3d b   do   do
Drips Jane, tailoress, N s 3d b   do   do
Dougherty Isabella, widow, N s 3d b   do   do
Davis Hugh, marshal W. Dist. Penn. office N s 4th b Market st and
     Jail alley, dw Allegheny town.
Daft Thomas, teacher, Birmingham.
Dennis James, nailor,   do
Davis David, coal-digger   do
Davis Jonathan, pudler, Kensington.
Davidson William, roller,   do
Denniston George, gate-keeper, Northern Liberties.
Danks Thomas, fireman,   do
Davis John, labourer,   do
Dazel James, carpenter,   do
Deely John, engineer,   do
Denvir Hugh, butcher, Allegheny town.
Dick David, labourer,   do
Dixon John, brick-maker,   do
Dill Francis, wagoner,   do
Dawson   stone-cutter   do

E

EVANS WILLIAM plane maker and music master, E s Irwin, b Penn
     and the Allegheny.
Evans David, carpenter, S E c of Liberty and 4th.
Ekin & Ledlie, com. merchants, N E c of Water and Market.
Ekin James, com. merchant, N s Front b Ferry and Redoubt al.
Eichbaum William, jr. post master, S s 2d b Market and Wood.
Earl Henry, merchant, W s Market b 4th and the Diamond.
Enoch Thomas, alderman, W s Diamond, S of Diamond al.
Engles Silas, printer, N s 3d b Market and Wood.
Eagal John, chair maker, S s Virgin al b Wood and Liberty.
Elliot Samuel, blacksmith, N E c Hay and Liberty.
Evans George, engineer, N W c Redoubt al and Water.
Ewart Jacob, blacksmith, N W c of Smithfield and 4th.
Evans Benjamin R. attorney, N s 4th n Liberty.
Ernest Frederick, clerk, N s Penn n Marbury.
Ebert George, clerk at Wm. D. Harris', Bayard's Row.
Evans Nancy, laundress, M'Masters' court.
Eddy Caleb, barber, W s Wood b 3d and 4th,
Edgar Jacob, carter, S s 5th b Wood and Smithfield.
Edgcumbe Henry, machine maker, N s Water b Wood and Market.
Ellis David, carpenter, N s Penn b Hand and Garrison alley.
Edmon Mary Ann, seamstress, S s Strawberry al n Liberty.
Eaton Samuel, labourer, S s Strawberry al b Smithfield and Liberty.
Eaton John   do   do   do   do
Elliott James W. blacksmith, N s 2d b Grant and Ross.
Evans Wm. water hauler, E s Grant b 2d and 3d.
Erwin John, carpenter W s Cherry al c of academy al.
Estep Joseph, grocer, c of Irwin and Liberty.

Evans Henry, laborer, W s Smithfield b 6th and Strawberry al.
Earle David, mason, S s Virgin al b Wood and Smithfield.
Edmon Samuel, laborer, S s Virgin al b Wood and Market.
Ekin & Ledlie, tobacco manufacturers, W's Ferry b Front and 2d.
Elder Fanny W. store keeper, S s Diamond al b Wood and Market.
Evans Mathias, carpenter, N s Penn b Marbury and Hay, dw at G. Morgan's.
Eichbaum Wm. sr. weigh master at the hay scales, dw N E c of Ferry and 3d.
Evans Richard, wrought nailor, Bowen's rolling mill.
Edwards Evan, shoemaker, Northern Liberties
Elias Robert, weaver   do
Ernest Byard, roller   do
Eichbaum Arnold, wire manufacturer, Kensington.
Evans Daniel, drayman   do
Ensell Charles, glass blower, Birmingham.
Ensell Edward, sen. do   do
Ensell Edward, jr. do   do
Evans Jobn,   do   do

F

FLEMING ROBERT, grocer, W s Liberty n the Monongahela.
Fleming Samuel, sawyer, W s Liberty n Bell's al.
Franklin Alexander, labourer, Point brewery.
Frisby Ephraim, ship carpenter, S s Penn, n Marbury.
Frisby Samuel,   do   do   do
Fleming Cochran, carter, W c of Marbury and Brewery al.
Francis Sarah, gentlewoman, S s Diamond al b Wood and Diamond.
Fairman Thomas, grocer, store N E c of 3d and Wood.
Forward Walter, Esq. S s Liberty b Cherry and Plumb al office N s 4th b Market and Jail al.
Fortune Walter, blacksmith, N s 4th b Wood and Smithfield.
Fosdick Ezekiel, last maker and grocer, S s 3d b Cherry al & Grant.
Ferguson David, blacksmith, shop S s 7th b Liberty and Smithfield, dw E s Smithfield b 7th and Virgin al.
Farrons John, tailor, W s Wood b Virgin al and 5th.
Faris George & Co. merchants, W s Market n 4th.
Fulton James, grocer, S s of the Diamond, E of Market.
Fleming Andrew, grocer, S W c of Grant and 2d.
Freeman John, moulder, W s Ross b Front and 2d.
Freeman Thomas, stone, earthen ware & fire brick maker, c of Grant and Cherry alley, dw W s Cherry b Pumb al and 7th.
Fearns William W. merchant, S s Diamond al, b Wood and market.
Fink Thomas, carpenter, and bellows maker, shop N s 5th b Wood & Hillsborough al, dw in Roseburg's Court.
Feilding John, shoemaker, N W c of Front and Smithfield.
Fielding William, weaver   do   do
Fetterman W. W. office c of Water and Redoubt al, dw N s Water b Market and Chancery lane.
Fox Michael, brush maker at George Beale's.
Fortune James, saddle-tree maker, N s 4th b Wood and Smithfield.
Fortune Luke   do   do   do

Fortune John, saddle-treee maker, at Walter Fortunes.
Foy Jesse, chandler, at Jackson's 4th st.
Fulton John, paper maker, in paper mill yard.
Fulton James C.   do   do
Fitzgerald Michael, labourer, S s Virgin al b Wood & Smithfield.
Fisher Rebecca, seamstress, S s 5th b Wood and Smithfield
Fochendor Mary, laundress, S s 5th do   do
Fluck Henry, blacksmith, W s Wood b 5th and Diamond al.
Franklin John, laborer, Barker's al n Allegheny.
French John, carter, E s Irwin b Penn and Allegheny.
Fair Catharine, tailoress, Maddock's alley.
Franklin William, Allegheny foundry, on M'Cormick's al.
Flemington Stewart, carpenter, Irwin's al n the Allegheny.
Fairman Mathew, stone cutter, N s Liberty b Wayne & Garrison al.
Fitzsimmons Nicholas, gent. S s of Strawberry al b Liberty & Smithf.
Fitzsimmons Andrew, bricklayer, W s of Smithfield b 7th and Straw-
    berry alley.
Fickner Adam, grocer, W s Liberty b Strawberry al and 7th.
Findlay William, grocer, N s Liberty b Hand and Garrison al.
Ford Hetty, shop keeper, E s Grant b 2d and 3d.
Frew Samuel, grocer, S E c of Liberty and Wood.
Freeman Jeptha, pressman, S s 3d b Grant and Ross.
Farly Thomas, carpenter, S W c of Ross and 3d.
Freeman Esther, N s 2d b Wood and Smithfield.
Frazier Daniel, labourer, N s 3d b do
Foulke Eliza, nurse, N s 2d n Ross.
Fitzsimmons & Read, merchants, No. 4, Bayard's Row.
Fitzsimmons David, merchant, E s Smithfield b 7th and Strawberry al.
Fitzsimmons William, gent. N s 3d b Wood and Smithfield.
Fisher Margaret, tailoress N s 6th b Church al and Smithfield.
Fanner Philip, carpenter, N W c of Strawberry and Miltenberger's al.
Fagan Thomas, labourer, S s 4th b Liberty and Ferry.
Forrester Nancy, gentlewoman, S s 4th b Ferry and Chancery lane.
Fitzsimmons Patrick, labourer, S E c of Front and Ferry.
Fullerton James, carter, N W c of Penn and Marbury.
Forbes Catharine, boarding house, S s 2d b Ferry and Chancery lane.
Fowler John, cabinet maker, S s 3d b Wood and Market.
Funston James, grocer, N s Diamond al b Wood and Diamond.
Fielding John H. teacher, E s Smithfield, b Strawberry al and 7th.
Fleming James, nailor, Birmingham.
Fields James, labourer   do
Flood William, do   do
Fulton Isabella, widow, Allegheny town.
Faulkner David, labourer   do
Forsyth James,   do   do
Fleming Hugh, Esq.   do
Faris Rachel, widow, Kensington.

G

GREGORY CHARLES, ship carpenter, S s Penn n Marbury.
Grant George, merchant, N s·Penn b Pitt and Hay.
Gray John B. high constable, S W c of 2d and Smithfield.
Graham William, jr. city treasurer, S s 4th n Smithfield.
Gormly James, sr. merchant, W c of Market and 5th.
Gormly William, gent. S W s of Diamond n Diamond al.
Grey James, gent. N s 4th b Market and Jail al.
Glass Walter, shoemaker, shop N s Liberty opposite to Wood, dw N
    W c of 6th and Smithfield.
Graham John, hatter, N s Diamond al n Wood.
Gray Moses, labourer, S E c of Marbury and Penn.
Glenn David, painter, S s 4th b Wood and Market.
Guthrie James V. constable, S s 2d n Market.
Gazzam Joseph, doctor, S s 4th n Wood.
Glass Robert, grocer, S W c of Strawberry al and Liberty.
Gray Joseph, turner, N s 4th n Wood.
Geer John, Captain, farrier, S s Diamond al n Wood.
Graham William, butcher, N s Diamond al b Wood and Smithfield.
Glenn Nathaniel, saddler, N E c of Wood and Diamond al.
Grant James, grocer, N W c of Diamond al and Diamond.
Griffith Nicholas, shoe and leather merchant, E s Wood b 3d & 4th.
Getty Richard, pump maker, N s 5th b Wood and Market.
Grier David, inkeeper, N s Liberty b Irwin's street & Irwin's al.
Gardner George, steward, N s 2d b Grant and Ross.
Gormly Andrew, merchant, N s Liberty n Hand.
Gibson James, labourer, E s of Irwin b Penn and Allegheny.
Gallagher John, brass founder, shop N s 2d b Wood and Smithfield.
    dw S s 3d b Wood and Smithfield.
Grier John, grocer S s Liberty b Wood and Strawberry al.
Green John, clerk at Robinson's glass house.
Gazzam Edward D. student at Richard Biddle's Esq.
Gallagher Daniel, brass founder, at John Gallagher's.
Greatrake Lawrence, Rev. N E c of Front and Smithfield.
Grierson Robert, merchant & shoemaker, S E c of Liberty & Market·
Glenn Charles, mason, W s Wood b 5th and Virginal.
Gay Daniel, merchant, S E c of Wood and Front.
Gardner James, labourer, S W c of 2d and Grant.
Gross Charles, blacksmith, S s Penn b Pitt and Stevenson's al.
Gill Elizabeth, seamstress, S s Penn b St. Clair and Cecil's al.
Garner Robert, laborer, E s Cecil's al n Allegheny.
Gallagher Patrick, labourer, N s 4th b Wood and Smithfield.
Gillespie Hamilton, weaver, M'Masters' Court.
Guisenhiemer Mary, widow, W s Wood b 5th and Diamond al.
Given's Samuel, shoe-maker, W s Irwin b Penn and Allegheny.
Givens Edward, carter   do   do   do
Gibson James, storekeeper, E s of Irwin b Penn and Allegheny.
Greer William, carter, M'Cormick's al
Grannis William, tobacconist, S W c of Garrison al and Penn.
Graham Thomas, labourer, S s Strawberry al b Liberty and Smithfield.
Gilleland Thomas, laborer, S W c of Liberty and Strawberry al.
George A. & S. grocers, N s of Liberty b Hand and Garrison al.

Gibson William, stone mason, S W c of Liberty and Plumb al.
Grafton Peter, water hauler, N s Grant b Front and Water.
Goldthorpe Joshua, fire brick maker, N s 2d b Ross and Grant.
Gray Thomas, painter, N s Watson's road, E of High st.
Gatt Thomas, labourer   do   do   do
Greenlea Mary, widow, N s Coal lane E of High.
Gallagher John, carter, E s Ross b 3d and 4th.
Gibson Joseph, labourer, N s Watson's road, n Ross.
Garwin James, carter, E side of Grant b 3d and 4th.
Gilchrist James, carpenter, N s Front b Grant and Cherry alley.
Gormly Sarah & Sisters, mantuamakers, N s Liberty opposite to Wood.
Green John, printer, at Johnston & Stockton's.
Gillespie Manassah, blacksmith, N E c of Smithfield and 5th.
Green Luke, labourer, W s church alley.
Givin Samuel, mason, N s Strawberry al b Smithfield and Miltenberger's alley.
Geddes John, labourer, E s Miltenberger's al.
Gamble John, Rev.   do   do
Gray Alexander, sexton, S E c Smithfield and 6th.
Gilleland James, labourer, E s Cherry al b 6th and Strawberry al.
Green William, labourer, S s Strawberry, b Cherry and Union alleys.
Graham Robert, carter, N s Strawberry, b Cherry & Miltenberger's al.
Gordon Robert, carter, W s Smithfield b 6th and Virgin al.
Gilland Rosamand, widow, W s of the Diamond, b Diamond al & Union.
Getty Andrew, carpenter, b Virgin al and 6th opposite Hoge's pond.
Gordon Marion, laundress, M'Clurg's Court.
Galbraith James, weaver, Harris' al.
Garner Thomas, weaver, Toman's Court.
Gordon Samuel, blacksmith, Killemoon's Court.
Gardner Michael, plough maker,   do
Gray John, tailor, N s 5th, b Wood and Smithfield.
Gayetty Peter J. merchant, S s 5th, b Wood and Market.
Gordon Elizabeth, laundress, W s Hillsborough al.
Glover James, weaver, S s Diamond al b Jail al and Liberty.
Gorman Theresa, gentlewoman, N s 4th, opposite to Ferry.
Gormly Samuel, attorney, office W s of the Diamond, n Union.
Glenn John, attorney, office E s Union.
Gormly & Matthews, merchants, W s Market, b 5th and Diamond.
Gormly James, jr.   do   do   do   do
Graham Thomas, domestic cotton manufacturer. W s Market b 5th & Liberty.
Gourly John, labourer, W s King's al.
Griffin Matthew, tobacconist, S s 2d, b Chancery lane and Ferry.
Glass Henry, labourer, E s Ferry, b Front and Water.
Griffin John, labourer, N E, c of Liberty and Marbury.
Gray Moses, labourer, N W c of Penn and Marbury.
Garner James, labourer   do   do
Goff William, gun smith, S s 2d b Wood and Market.
Gilchrist Robert, hatter, N s 3d do   do
Griffen James, clerk, at the Recorder's office.
Gibb John, chemist, Northern Liberties.
Getty Mary, widow   do
Glass David, shoemaker   do

Gibson William, stone cutter N. Liberties.
Gano John, gent. do
Gates William, hammerman, do
Glenn David, shoemaker, Birmingham.
Glenn John, labourer, do
Gallagher James, shoemaker do
Greenough Thomas, gent. Kensington.
Galbreath Robert, engineer, do
Graham William, roller, do
Gallagher Hugh, moulder, Allegheny town.
Gray James, gent. do
Graham Foster, carpenter do
Gazzam Ann, widow do
Graham William, plasterer do
Gray Richard, brickmaker do
Graham Willam, brick moulder do
Graham Martha, widow do
Guyer Jacob, butcher do

H

HEALD JOHN S. Gold & Silversmith, N s 2d opposite Post office
Haughy Daniel, grocer, E s Liberty, n the Ferry.
Henderson Jane, nurse, S s Penn, n Marbury.
Hutchinson H. G. turner, W s Market, b 4th and Diamond.
Hutchinson Wm. inkeeper, S s 5th b Wood and Market.
Hutchinson Joseph, do do 3d b Wood and Smithfield.
Hutchinson Lewis, com. merchant, N s Liberty, b Pitt and Cecil's al.
Hamilton James, labourer, N s 2d b Wood and Smithfield.
Holmes Sheply R. doctor, S s 5th b Wood and Market.
Hoge Mary, widow, W s Smithfield b 3d and 4th.
Henderson Archibald, sexton, S s 6th b Church al and Wood.
Haslet Wm. carter, S s Virgin al b Wood and Smithfield.
Herron John, miller and lumber merchant, N E c of Irwin's alley and
    Penn.
Holdship Henry, book store, N W c of Wood and 3d, dw N s 3d n
    Smithfield.
Herron Francis Rev. N W c of Wayne and Penn.
Hays William, tanner, yard c of Jail al and Liberty, dw N E c of Penn
    and Pitt.
Hatch Ebenezer, lumber merchant, E s Smithfield b 6th and Straw-
    berry al.
Harshaw John, bricklayer, W s Cherry al n 6th.
Hunter Daniel, gent. N s 2d b Cherry al and Grant.
Holmes Nat. broker & porter merchant, W s Market, b 2d and 3d.
Hazelton Mary, store keeper, S s Diamond al b Wood and Market.
Hannen John, Esq. N s 6th b Wood and Smithfield.
Hague Reuben, carpenter, S s Strawberry al b Cherry alley and
    Smithfield.
Hazlet Robert, weaver, S W c of Liberty and Plumb al.
Harris Isaac, merchant, store N E c of Market and 5th, dw S s Penn,
    b Wayne and Garrison alley.

Hays Wm. H. iron merchant, E s High, n Coal lane.
Harmon James, shoemaker, W s Wood b 2d and 3d.
Haslet Joseph, gent. N E c of Wood and 5th.
Hart Scudder, trader, N E c of 3d and Ferry.
Hegan James, tailor, S s of 5th b Union and Liberty.
Hubly Samuel, inkeeper, N W c of Ferry and Front.
Hamill James, carpenter, N s 7th b Cherry al and Grant.
Heisner Henry, baker and inkeeper, S E c of Smithfield & Virgi , al.
Holmes Walter R. plasterer, E s Carpenter's al n Virgin al.
Hart William H. toll receiver, at the Monongahela bridge.
Holmes Nathaniel, porter merchant, S s 3d b Wood and Market.
Hare Francis, water hauler, S s 5th b Wood and Smithfield.
Harvy H. A. grocer, No. 3, Gray's Row.
Horn Frederick, gent N W c of 5th and Church al.
Hartupie William, blacksmith, shop bank of Allegheny, on Cecil's al.
     dw N s Liberty, b St. Clair and Cecil's al.
Holdship George, carpenter, S s 5th b Wood and Market.
Hart S. & A. freighters, E s Wood, b Front and Water.
Hart Aaron, dw W s Smithfield, b 2d and 3d.
Hopkins Solomon, gent. Carpenter's alley, n Virgin alley.
Hill Isaac, inkeeper, S E c of Virgin al and Wood.
Herrington M. clerk, N W c of Garrison al and Penn.
Harris Stephen, shoemaker, E s Wood b Front and Water.
Hunter Thomas, clerk, at Evans' steam mill, dw W s Ferry n 2d.
Headrick David, woollen manufacturer, S W c of Liberty and Diam-
     ond alley.
Henry David, ferryman, at Speers' ferry.
Hubly Samuel, carpenter, at Samuel Hubly's
Hilton William, at Kay's tavern, Union st.
Holdship George W. clerk, at Holdship's bookstore.
Hazelton Samuel, jr. grocer, N s Diamond, n Market.
Harris Wm. D. merchant, No. 3, Bayard's Row.
Hamitt James, shoemaker, W s of Smithfield, b Front and 2d.
Howard & Rogers, coppersmiths and tinners, N W c of 2d and Wood,
Howard Wm. coppersmith, dw   do   do   do
Holmes Albert E. dancing master, S s 2d b Wood and Market.
Horn Abraham, sen. baker, S s Penn, b St. Clair and Cecil's al.
Horn   do   jr.   do   do   do   do
Hibbet Joseph, hosier, S s Penn n Cecil's al.
Hunter James, printer, S s Diamond al, b Wood and Smithfield.
Hunter Robert, weaver, M'Masters' Court.
Hague Stephen, hatter, W s Wood b Diamond al and 4th.
Hamilton Eleanor, milliner, S s 4th b Wood and Market.
Hanson John, grocer, W s Wood b 5th and Diamond al.
Hollingsworth Hannah, widow, S s 5th b Wood and Smithfield.
Humphrey Robert, labourer,   do   do   do
Horner John, druggist, N E c of 3d and Market.
Hazelton Hugh, coroner and whitesmith, shop W s Wood b 6th and
     Virgin al, dw N s Liberty, n Cecil's al.
Holdship William, shoemaker, N s Penn b Irwin st. and Barker's al.
Highfield John, labourer, E s Irwin b Penn and the Allegheny.
Hively Michael, sen. cooper, Maddock's al.
Hively Michael, jr. labourer,   do

Herron Francis, weaver, Maddock's al.
Hughen Robert, labourer,   do
Hare James, labourer, M'Cormick's al.
Hays Robert, labourer, S s Penn, b Hand and Garrison al.
Hill Robert, cooper, S s Strawberry al b Liberty and Smithfield.
Hughes Edward, shoemaker, S s   do   do
Hanna Thomas, labourer, S s   do   do
Hodge Eliza, seamstress, W s Smithfield, b Strawberry al and 6th.
Hunter Esther, widow, N s Water b Grant and Ross.
Hutton Isaiah, tanner, E s Grant b Water and Front.
Halfpenny John, shoemaker, S s Front b Grant and Ross.
Hurl John, drayman, N s 2d b   do
Hall Nancy, inkeeper, N s 2d b   do
Harsly Augustus, ship carpenter, N s 2d b   do
Harrison Joseph, weaver, E s Grant b 2d and 3d.
Harris David, labourer, E s   do   do
Harris Mary, teacher, E s   do   do
Howard Mary, tailoress, S E c of Grant and 3d.
Hurst Caleb, carpenter, N s 3d b Grant and Ross.
Holmes Enoch, millwright, E s Grant b 3d and 4th.
Howell Sarah, mantua maker, N s Water b Cherry al & Smithfield.
Hay John, glass blower, N s Front b Grant and Cherry al.
Hay Alexander, carpenter, N s 3d do   do   do
Hawdon Michael, blacksmith, S s do   do   do
Hemingray William, grocer, W s Smithfield, n 2d
Hartley Thomas, dyer, E s Wood b 5th and Diamond al.
Haines Levi, grocer, N E c of Front and Smithfield.
Huff Amos, shoemaker, N s Front b Smithfield and Cherry al.
Hively Elizabeth, laundress, N s Water, b Wood and Smithfield.
Harris Susan   do   do   do   do
Haslet Elizabeth, tailoress, do   do   do
Hastings Abel, tailor, N s 2d b Wood and Smithfield.
Hunter John, book binder, N s 3d b Wood and Smithfield.
Hughes John, labourer, S s 3d   do   do
Holmes David, grocer, S s Liberty b Market and Virgin al.
Hunter David, carter, N s Liberty b Irwin's st. and Irwin's al.
Hedger James, blue dyer, E s church al.
Holmes Abraham, hatter,   do   do
Hazlet William, labourer, W s   do
Holmes Edward E. plasterer, W s Smithfield, b 6th & Strawberry al.
Holmes Robert, labourer, W s   do   do   do
Hamilton James G. labourer, W s   do   do   do
Holdship Sarah, shoe binder, do   do   do   do
Holmes Abigal, gentlewoman do   do   do   do
Hastings Mathew, labourer, N s Strawberry al, b Smithfield and Cherry alley.
Hart John, hammerman, N W c of Strawberry and Miltenberger's al.
Hull Margaret, laundress, E s Smithfield b 6th and Strawberry al.
Hening Samuel, weaver, S s 7th b Cherry al and Grant.
Hobson John, fuller, W s Grant b 7th and Strawberry al.
Hodge Jane, storekeeper, N W c of Smithfield and Virgin al.
Howe William, hatter, E s Smithfield, b 6th   do
Hamilton Jane, widow, E s Smithfield, b 6th and Virgin al

Hilton Ann, milliner, E s of Wood b 5th and Virgin al.
Hinds John, hatter, N s Water, b Ferry and Chancery lane.
Hilton Wm. teacher, E s Wood b 5th and Virgin al.
Hany James, blacksmith   do   do
Haly William, coach maker, S s Virgin al, b Wood and Market.
Heartzall Jemima, widow, school mistress, Jail al n Liberty.
Hartman Henry, moulder, S W c of Liberty and Jail alley.
Hamblin William, hatter, E s Jail al n 4th.
Humbert Margaret, boarding house, N s 4th b Jail al and Liberty.
Hilbert Catharine, tailoress, N s   do   do   do
Hannen John & Son, druggists, W s Market b 5th and Liberty.
Hannen Henry, doctor, shop   do   do   do   dw S s
    5th b Wood and Smithfield.
Hughes James, stone cutter, N E c of Liberty and Virgin al.
Hall William, blacksmith, W s King's al.
Horn Henry, shoemaker, E s   do
Hanson James, saddler, S E c of Redoubt al and 2d.
Hanson & Brice, do   S W c of Market and 2d.
Holland Edward, tailor, E s Ferry b Front and 2d.
Hancock Richard, boarding house, N s Front b Wood and Market
Hamilton William, carpenter, E s Wood b Front and 2d.
Hukill James, shoemaker, E s Marbury b Penn and Liberty.
Harper Henry, laborer, N s Liberty b Hay and Marbury.
Harper Robert, loom maker   do   do
Hawk James, shoemaker, S s 2d b Market and Chancery lane.
Holmes A. G. dentist, S s 2d b Wood and Market.
Hare Jane, shop keeper, N s Diamond al b Diamond and Wood.
Holland William, skiff builder, N s Front b Wood and Smithfield.
Hern John, painter, N s 3d b Wood and Market.
Hill Gasper, teacher, S s do   do
Hanson Jacob, auctioneer, at Davis & Hanson's.
Hunter Eliza, teacher, W s Ferry b 2d and 3d.
Hughes Richard, grocer, E s of the Diamond S of Diamond al.
Hall William, engineer, shop at Suke's run, n 2d, dw in Kensington
Hurlbert Robert W. saddle-tree plater, S s 5th b Wood and Smithfield.
Hetherington Robert, waterman, Kensington.
Hughes Lewis, pudler   do
Harden John, carpenter   do
Hoover Henry, labourer, Northern Liberties
Hamilton William, stone mason   do
Hamilton John, weaver   do
Hastings John, tailor   do
Haslet John, teacher   do
Hook Israel, blacksmith   do
Hunter James, labourer   do
Herron John, cannon borer   do
Hull John, rope-maker, Allegheny town.
Herron William, mason   do
Hackett John, carpenter   do
Heckesweller Jacob, potter   do
Hulings Samuel, freighter, Birmingham.
Hare Samuel, Esq.   do

Hodgman Mary, seamstress, Birmingham.
Hart John, potter   do
Hait Isaac, labourer   do
Hain Frederick, glass blower, do
Hartman Jacob, founder   do

I

IRWIN JOHN, gent. N E c of Market and 4th.
Irwin William, grocer, S s Diamond al b Wood and Market.
Israel Charles H. attorney at law, office S s 3d b Wood and Market—
    dw in Front st c of Redoubt alley.
Irwin John, grocer, E s Wood b 6th and Liberty.
Irwin Robert, grocer, N s of Liberty b Irwin st and Irwin's alley.
Irwin William F. doctor, E s Wood, 2d door above Diamond alley.
Irwin Jane, milliner, west s Wood b 6th and Liberty.
Irwin John, rope-maker, warehouse c of Redoubt alley and Liberty st.
    dw in Allegheny town.
Irwin Martha, gentlewoman, N W c of Penn st and Irwin's alley.
Irwin James, carpenter,   do   do   do
Irwin James, drayman, E s Grant b 3d and 4th.
Irwin James, currier, S E c of Diamond and Market st.
Irwin Sarah, widow,   do   do   do
Israel Joseph, bricklayer, Miltenberger's alley.
Ingraham Wm. butcher, S s Virgin alley b Wood and Liberty st
Ings Elizabeth, tailoress, S s 3d b Market and Wood.
Irwin John S. doctor, S s Liberty, b 6th st and Virgin alley.
Irwin John, carpenter, c of Academy and Cherry alley.
Impson Charles, glass-blower, Birmingham.
Irwin Joshua,   do   do
Irwin Christopher, brick-maker,   do
Irwin Mary, gentlewoman, Allegheny town
Irwin Joseph, carpenter   do
Irwin Margaret, widow, N. Liberties.

J

JONES SARAH, widow, c of Bell's alley and Penn st.
Johnston Samuel, labourer, Point, old garrison.
Jennings Peter, butcher, Brewery alley n Marbury st.
Jackman Andrew, carter, W s of Irwin b Penn and the Allegheny.
Jones Rees, tobacconist, S E c of Penn and Hand.
Jones Rees, Jr. do   do   do   do
Jackson George W. grocer, S W c of Diamond and Market st.
Jackson John, chandler, S s of Diamond 2d door W of Market.
Johnston John, grocer, S s Diamond alley, b Wood and Market.
Johnston & Stockton, booksellers and printers, W s Market b 2d and
    3d.   Johnston S. R. dw   do   do   do
Jones John, bricklayer, N s Diamond al b Wood and Market.
Johnston William, tailor, E s Wood, b 4th st and Diamond al.
Jackson George, grocer, N s 5th b Wood and Smithfield.

11 *

Johnston Alexander, Jr. cashier of the Bank of Pittsburgh, S W c of Market and 3d.

Jenkins John, pattern maker, carver, &c. Stewart's court.

Jones Lydia, widow, S s 3d b Wood and Smithfield.

Jones Samuel, conveyancer, S s 4th E of Market.

Jack Robert, carpenter, E s Cecil's alley, b Wood and Smithfield.

Jones Joshua, bricklayer, N s Diamond al b Wood and Smithfield.

Jones Mary, widow,   do   do   do

Jackson Benjamin, grocer, Water, b Wood and Market.

Jack & Short, coppersmiths and tinners, N E c of Wood and Water.

Jack Henry,   do   dw Water b Wood and Market.

James Jesse, paper-maker, in paper mill yard.

James Richard, glass-engraver, N s Water b Grant and Ross.

Johnston Gerardus, carpenter, Maddock's alley.

Joyce Patrick, weaver,   do   do

Johnston Francis, labourer, High st.

Jackson Ralph, farrier, Water b Cherry al and Smithfield.

Jones Edward, clerk, Water, b Grant and Cherry al.

Johnston George, water-hauler, S s Front b Grant st and Cherry al.

Johnston Mary, widow, S s 3d b   do   do

Johnston Samuel, shoeblack, Academy alley.

James Wm. tailor, S W c of Liberty st and Virgin al.

Jenkinson Joseph, painter, N s 6th b Wood st and Church alley.

Jones Elizabeth, tailoress, N s Strawberry alley b Smithfield and Miltenberger's alley.

Jewel David, constable, E s Smithfield b Strawberry al and 7th st.

Johnston Elizabeth, laundress, S s Strawberry b Cherry and Foster's alleys.

Johnston Lucy, seamstress, west s Grant, b 7th and Strawberry al.

Johnson Francis, weaver, Carpenter's alley.

Johnston Hezekiah, captain, c of Garrison al and Penn st.

Johnston Henry S. teacher, S s Virgin al b Wood and Smithfield.

Johnston John, cooper,   do   do   do   do

Jameson Robert, weaver, Hillsborough alley.

Jenkins Mary, seamstress, N s 4th b Liberty st and Jail alley.

Jester Elijah, chairmaker, S s Liberty, b Virgin al and 6th st.

Johnston William, cooper, E s King's alley.

Johnston W. shoemaker, back from 5th b Wood and Market.

Jope John W. wire-worker, S s 2d b Market and Wood.

Jardell Alexis, glass-engraver, west s Wood b 2d and 3d.

Jackson William Turner, W s Smithfield, b Front and Water.

Jones Thomas, coal-digger, Kensington.

Jones Joseph, labourer,   do

Jones Thomas, weigh-man, N. Liberties.

Johnston Thomas, esq.   do

Jourdan Samuel, grocer,   do

Jones Robert, engineer,   do

Johnston Joseph, bridge-builder, Allegheny town.

Jones N. S. shoe and boot-maker,   do

Johnston John, late post master,   do

Jones Evan, coal-digger, Birmingham.

Jones Thomas, ferryman, on the Monongahela, opposite the mouth of Liberty st.

Jones Marshal, trader, at Th. Jones' ferry.
Jones Ephraim, captain, at Mrs. Bracken's.

K

KINTZER GEORGE, innkeeper and ferryman S W end of Liberty street.
Kingsland Lawrence, High street.
Kingston Samuel, attorney at law, N E c of the Diamond.
Knox Miss Nancy, S s 5th, E of Market.
Kelly John, trader, S s Front b Ferry st and Chancery lane.
Kerr Andrew L. grocer, N E corner of Hand and Liberty.
Kurtz Rev. Henry, S E c of Smithfield st and Strawberry alley.
Knox Robert, baker, N side of Front, just above Wood.
Kerr Ebenezer, innkeeper, Union street.
Kinsey Samuel, boat builder, Water, b Wood and Market.
King David, merchant, Denniston's hotel.
Kaye Joshua, innkeeper, Union st.
Konecke Richard N. merchant, W s Market, b 4th and Diamond.
Kelly William, student, at Dr. Holmes'
Kirkpatrick Matthew, at Davis and Hanson's auc.
Kennedy W. Carpenter, E s Cecil's alley b Penn and the Allegheny.
Kerns Anthony, cooper, N E corner of Penn st and Cecil's alley
Kirkpatrick Alexander, labourer, N s Diamond al b Wood and Smithf.
Kinkead David, tailor, E s Wood 3d door below Diamond al.
Kramer Allen, hatter, W s Wood b 4th st and   do
Keys Adam, labourer, S s 5th b Wood and Smithfield.
Kennedy Michael, grocer, S side of Diamond W of Market st.
Keefer Samuel W. tobacconist, N s of do   E of Union st.
Kirkpatrick Thomas, painter, Garrison alley, b Penn and Liberty.
King John, flour and feed store, N side Liberty above Hand.
Kendal John, shoemaker, N s 2d b Grant and Ross.
Kendal Joseph, boat-builder, do   do   do
Kain Nancy, nurse, No. 2 Gray's Row.
Kennedy Margaret, laundress, E s Grant, b 2d and 3d.
Kidd Elsa, widow, S s 3d b Grant and Ross.
Kelty Arthur, blacksmith, W s Ross, b 2d and 3d.
Kennedy Robert, moulder, E s Grant b 3d and 4th.
Klinefelter Henry, carpenter, N s Front, b Wood and Smithfield.
Keller William   do   do   do   do
Kirkpatrick Mathew, labourer, Church alley.
Kelly Charles, grocer, Water just above Ferry.
Knox James, bricklayer, Carpenter's alley.
Kingsland Phillip, Moulder, E s Smithfield, b Virgin al and 5th.
Kennedy Stephen, shoemaker S s Virgin alley b Wood and Smithf.
Kennedy Samuel, carter,   do   do   do
Kerwin Mary Ann, store-keeper, E s of Market b 3d and 4th.
Knowles Wm. gentlemen, E s Market b Front and Water.
Kelly Rachel, midwife, at Read's inn, 5th st.
Kidd Mary, seamstress, Miltenberger's court.
Knox James, freighter, N W c of 3d and Chancery lane.
Keller Samuel, iron merchant, S s of Front b Market and Wood.

Knox Isabella, teacher, N W c of 3d st and Chancery lane.
Kinkead Phill'p, plough-maker, S s 2d b Ferry st and Chancery lane.
Kinkead James, tinner,   do   do   do
Keatting Hugh, drayman, S W corner of 3d and Ferry.
Kitts Job, grocer, S s Diamond alley, b Wood st and Diamond.
Kesler Margaret, Shop-keeper, W s St. Clair b Penn and Liberty.
Kerr James, carpenter, S s 3d b Grant st and Cherry alley.
Kennedy David, labourer, Birmingham.
Kinkead Thomas, tanner,   do
Knox William, waterman, Allegheny town.
Kune John, labourer,   do
Kune James, do   do
Kune Thomas, do   do
Kerr Rev. Joseph,   do
Kerr Martin, shoemaker,   do
Kerr Samuel, teacher,   do
Kearney Patrick, labourer,   do
Krouse Christian, butcher, N. Liberties.
Kerns John, grocer,   do
Kelly Abraham, chandler,   do

L

LENT ANDREW, ship-carpenter, N W c of Marbury and Liberty.
Lecky Robert, wagon and coach-maker, N W c of Virgin al & Wood.
Lecky William, Sheriff, office in court-house, dw Allegheny town.
Logan David, com. merchant, c of Ferry and Water.
Long Joseph, blacksmith, W s Ferry b 3d and 4th.
Lindell Robert, com. merchant, N E c of 2d and Ferry.
Liggett John, cabinet maker, N s Front b Wood and Smithfield.
Liggett James, do   do W s of Wood, b Front and 2d.
Lowrie & Curtis, grocers, W s Wood b 3d and 4th.
Lowrie M. B. alderman, N s 2d b Wood and Market.
Logan Francis, drayman, S s 4th b Wood and Smithfield.
Lusk John,   do   do   do   do
Little John, saddler, shop, c of Market and Water, dw S s 2d a few
     doors E of Market.
Leech Malcolm, grocer, S s Liberty, b Wood st and Strawberry alley,
     dw N s 7th b Smithfield and Cherry alley.
Lewis Richard, carpenter, N s 6th b Church alley and Smithfield st.
Lappin Mrs. widow, N s Penn, b Irwin's street and Maddock's al.
Lutz Frederick, painter, N s 2d b Wood and Smithfield.
Leonard Patrick, grocer, S E corner of the Diamond.
Lee Caleb, draper and tailor, E s Market, b 4th and Diamond.
Ledlie George, com. mer. dw N s Liberty just above Marbury.
Liggett Thomas, carpenter, S s 2d b Wood and Smithfield.
Leyburn John, carpenter, S s 3d b   do   do
Leech John, grocer, E s Market b 5th st and Diamond.
Lyndsay Robert, turner, S s of Virgin alley, n Liberty.
Lynch & Lope, grocers, W s of Wood b Front and Water.
Lappin James & Co. merchants, W side of Market, 3d door N of 4th.
Loomis Luke, clerk, at Holdship's bookstore.

Lucky George, carpenter, and gold and silver-smith, S s Diamond al.
    b Wood and Market.
Lightcap Solomon, Innkeeper, N W c of Wood st and Diamond al'
Love Wm. whitesmith, at Th. Hazelton's.
Lee Louisa, tailoress, N s Front, b Wood and Smithfield.
Lyons Wm. clerk, E s Pitt n the Allegheny.
Lowrie James, cooper, S s 5th b Wood and Smithfield.
Leslie Jane, gentlewowan, do   do   do
Lyons Peggy, seamstress, do   do   do
Lawrence Anthony, barber, Water b Wood and Market.
Linton John, gent.   do   do   do
Lutzenberger Henry, shoemaker, S s Penn b St. Clair and Cecil's al.'
Litle Henry, carpenter, Barker's alley, n the Allegheny.
Lemmox James, labourer, N E c of Penn st and Barker's alley.
Leonard Dennis, cooper, N s of Penn n   do   do
Lewis Allen, weaver, E s Irwin between Penn and the Allegheny
Loughry John, tobacconist, S s Strawberry, b Liberty and Smithf
Leonard Samuel, iron turner, S s 7th b Cherry al and Smithfield.
Levis Richard, labourer, Bakewell's court.
Lawler James, glass-blower, do   do
Lapp Joseph, drayman, Water b Grant and Ross.
Lewis Elizabeth, nurse, do   do   do
Lyndsay Ann, laundress, do   do   do
Lewis Samuel, roller, S s 2d b   do   do
Lurkins Thomas, blacksmith, N s 2d b do   do
Lusk William, labourer, S E c of Cherry al. and Front st.
Laird Robert, tailor, S s 3d b Cherry al and Grant st..
Lewis Abraham, shoeblack, W side Wood, b 2d and 3d.
Lephart Andrew, blacksmith, Irwin's alley, b Penn and Liberty.
Lane Mary, laundress, Church alley.
Leyburn James, carpenter, N E c of 6th and Church alley.
Lewis David, laborer, N s Strawberry b Smithfield st and Miltenber-
    gers alley.
Ludlow Wm. labourer, E s Smithfield b 7th and Strawberry alley.
Love Harmon, miller, W s Smithfield, b 6th and Virgin alley.
Lanfesty John, cooper, N s Front b Wood and Smithfield.
Lynch David, tobacconist, S s Front W of Wood.
Litle Mary, widow, S s 6th b Smithfield st and Cherry alley.
Litle Martin, glass-blower, do   do   do
Leonard James, shopkeeper, Jail alley.
Leonard James Jr. bricklayer, do
Lightner Isaac, at Jackson Foundry, dw Allegheny town.
Little Miss Mary, milliner, E s Market b 3d and 4th.
Loyd & O'Neal, saddlers, do   do   do
Loyd Alfred,   do   dw S s Front n Wood.
Ledlie Margaret, widow, W s Ferry b Front and 2d.
Lewis Peter, hatter, N s Front b Wood and Market.
Licken William, drayman, and grocer, N s Liberty b Marbury & Hay.
Leyburn Wm. & John, cabinet makers, N s 3d b Wood and Market.
Lennox Andrew, gunsmith, next door to post office.
Laughran John, labourer, Kensington.
Lee John,   do   do
Laughran Patrick, carter,   do

Love Frederick, labourer, Kensington.
Leonard Reuben, roller,   do
Leonard Phillip, forgeman,   do
Lowe John, carder,   N. Liberties.
Lowrie Mark, butcher,   do
Leech Dugald cotton spinner, do
Linton Jeremiah, butcher,   do
Lindsay James,   do
Little John, carpenter,   do
Leslie Alex. rope-maker, Allegheny town.
Leslie Thomas do   do
Lindsay Isabel, widow,   do

M

MORTON ANDREW, grocer, E s Liberty, c of Liberty and Front.
Magee Mary, laundress, Penn n Marbury.
Miller William, rigger, *W* s Marbury n Penn.
Miller Robert, labourer, N s of Liberty b Marbury and Bell's al.
Milligan Hugh, carter, E s Marbury n Liberty.
Milligan William, carpenter, E s Marbury n Liberty.
Mason Archibald, carpenter, shop *W* s Smithfield, b Front & Water,
     dw N E c of High and Watson's road.
Mowry Peter, doctor, E s of the Diamond, N of Diamond al.
Magnier Peter, barber, *W* s of the Diamond, b Diamond al & Union.
Martin William, shoemaker, N s 4th b Wood and Smithfield.
Magee Christopher, hatter, shop E s of Market b 2d and 3d, dw N *W*
     c of Chancery lane and Front.
Morse David, nailor, S s Diamond al n Smithfield.
Morse Gilbert, sprig and sparable maker, shop *W* s Wood b Virgin
     alley and 6th.
Miltinberger George, coppersmith & tinner, S E c of Market & Front.
Marshall John, gent. S s 4th below Cherry alley.
Minnis James, tinner, S s Penn b St. Clair st and Cecil's alley.
Mitchell John, cook, S s 3d b Grant and Ross.
Marshall John, blacksmith, W s Smithfield, b 4th and Diamond al.
Moore James, cabinet maker, N s 2d b Wood and Market.
Moore Edward, brass founder, E s Smithfield b 5th and Virgin al.
Melvin Philip, messenger, at the bank of Pittsburgh.
Murphy Dennis, grocer, N W c of Front and Wood.
Meek John, trader, N s Liberty b Irwin's st and Irwin's al.
Mulvany Patrick, cabinet maker, E s Market b Front and 2d.
Mason & M'Donough, wholesale merchants, E s of Wood b 3d and 4th.
Mason M. S. merchant, dw   do   do   do
Murray Magnus M. alderman, office S s of the Diamond W of Market,
     dw N s of Penn b Marbury and Hay.
Miskelly William, grocer, N s Diamond al b Wood and Market.
Martin Thomas, merchant, S s Liberty b Wood and Strawberry al.
Macky Samuel, inkeeper, W s of the Diamond n Union st.
Mitchell Lawrence, tailor, S W c of 2d and Wood.
Morgan Gideon, watchmaker, W s Wood b 2d and 3d.
Martin Adam, labourer, N s 4th b Jail al and Market.

Morford James, wagon and plough maker, S s Penn b Irwin & Hand.
Mercer John, grocer, S W c of Ferry and 2d.
Miller & Jenkins, pattern & plough makers shop at Jackson foundry.
Miller Timothy, plough maker, E s Hillsborough n 5th.
Macky James, constable, E s Redoubt al b 3 and 4th.
Mullin William, innkeeper, N s Water b Ferry and Chancery lane.
Morrison Henry, tailor, W s Wood b 3d and 4th.
Marshall John, carpenter, S s 4th b Smithfield and Cherry al.
Myers John V. clerk, at Wm. M'Knight's store.
Mitchell Benj. tailor, W s Wood b Front and Water.
Miller & Wilson, merchants, W s Wood b Front and 2d.
Miller Reuben, dw N s 2d b Wood and Smithfield.
Morse Benjamin, domestic coffee maker, S s Diamond al b Wood and
     Smithfield.
Murphy Wiliam C. cabinet maker, S s 4th b Wood and Smithfield.
Mitchell William, tailor, shop E s Market b 2d and 3d.
Maxwell Samuel, shoemaker, shop W s Wood b 4th and Diamond al.
Maxwell John,   do   do   do   do   do   do
Mountain A. S. T. attorney, N s Liberty b St. Clair and Cecil's al.
Morrison Hugh, blacksmith, Bowen's al.
Maclean David & Matthew, printers and editors of the Pittsburgh Ga-
     zette, S s 4th b Market and Wood.
Maclean David, printer, dw S s 4th b Market and Wood.
Mackey Robert, saddler, E s Wood b 5th and Diamond al.
Miller Joseph, laborer, E s Wood b 5th and Virgin al.
Murphy John, blacksmith, shop W s Wood b 5th and Diamond al, dw
     S s Virgin al b Wood and Smithfield.
Magee John, cooper, shop E s St. Clair b Penn and Liberty, dw No. 2
     Gray's Row.
Mills David, Fireman, Adams' alley.
Magee Patrick, cooper,   do
Murry Patrick, cooper, W s Irwin b Penn and Allegheny
Murphy James, weaver, E s Irwin b Penn and Allegheny
Moore James, cooper   do   do   do
Mackonnell John, labourer, E s do   do
Mason William, carpenter, Maddock's alley.
Mooney James, labourer   do
Morrow Robert, engineer, Irwin's al.
Mackie James, grocer, N W c of Penn and Hand.
Mazurie Sarah, S s Penn b Hand and Garrison al..
Munion Terrence, labourer N s of Penn b Garrison al and Wayne.
Morrow William, captain, S s Strawberry al b Liberty and Smithfield.
Morrow Susan, widow   do   do   do
Mullin William, shoemaker   do   do   do
Martin Samuel, labourer   do   do   do
Means Patrick, weaver, W s Smithfield b Strawberry al and 7th,
Means Charles, blacksmith   do   do
Miller William, shoemaker, shop S W c of 7th and Smithfield, dw E s
     Jail al b Diamond al and Liberty.
Murphy James, laborer, N E c of Garrison al and Liberty.
Murdock James, carpenter, N s Liberty b Garrison al and Wayne.
Martin William, mason, S s Penn   do   do
Morrison John, drayman N s Front b Market and Wood.

Miller Mary, laundress, N E c of Garrison al and the Allegheny.
Mullin George, laborer, Fayette al.
Melingen Jacob, pattern maker, N s of 7th b Smithfield and Cherry al.
Moore Martha, shop keeper, S s Front b Grant and Ross.
Mahie Samuel, master teazer, S s   do   do
Maizlaind George, clerk, N s Front   do   do
Moliere William, nailor, N s do   do   do
Milburn Thomas, labourer, E s High st.
Moreland Robert, labourer, S s Front c of Bakewell's al.
Mewhorny Hannah, laundress, N s Front b Smithfield and Cherry al.
Miller Amherst, ceder cooper, N E c of Water and Smithfield.
Mackie Arthur, water hauler, Redoubt alley b 3d and Liberty.
Merryman James, blacksmith, N s 2d b Wood and Smithfield.
Martin William, carter, N s 3d b Wood and Smithfield.
Martin Sarah, tailorless do   do   do
Means Robert, engineer, Chancery lane.
Mullin Michael, grocer, No. 6, Bayard's Row.
Mansell Joseph, baker, N s Liberty, b Irwin's st. and Irwin's al.
Majerkins Charles, shoemaker, E s Irwin b Penn and Liberty.
Mann Elizabeth, milliner, N s Irwin's al b Liberty and Penn.
Meynar Nicholas P. shoemaker, N s 6th above Church al.
Miller Robert, weaver, Miltenberger's alley.
Marshall John, stone cutter, do
Moorhead Thomas, water-hauler, N s Strawberry, b Cherry and Mil-
      tenberger's alley.
Mooney James, labourer, W s   do   do   do
Mackarel James, carpenter, S E c of Carpenter's alley and 6th st.
Miller Mrs. J. midwife, Water, b Wood and Market.
Morris J. boot and shoemaker, E s Smithfield, b Virgin al. and 5th.
Mackarihn Thomas, labourer, S s Virgin al b Wood and Smithfield.
May Patrick, weaver,   do   do   do   do
Mann George, gunsmith, Killemoon's court.
Merryman David, blacksmith, S c of Virgin and King's alley.
Meeker Ellen, boarding house, S s 3d b Wood and Market.
Marange John, nailor, S s Liberty, b Jail and Diamond alley.
Murphy Isaac, attorney at law, Union street.
Matthews James, merchant, S s 4th b Ferry and Chancery lane.
Mullin Wm. grocer, S E c of Market and Liberty streets.
Means Wm. shoemaker, S s Liberty, b Virgin alley and 6th st.
Morrow Jane, widow, N s 5th b Wood and Market.
Morrison Joseph, tailor, E s Market, b 3d and 4th.
Mills Andrew, shoemaker, W s Market b Front and Water.
Miller Michael, ship carpenter, W s Ferry b 2d and 3d.
Morton James, trader, E s Ferry b Front and 2d.
Murray James, water hauler, E s Ferry b Front and Water.
Miller Ann, shop keeper, N s Water b Ferry and Redoubt al.
Means Martha, nurse, Chancery lane, b Front and Water.
Murphy John, labourer, S W c of Front and Chancery lane.
Miller & Robinson, tobacco manufactory, Chancery lane b Front & 2d.
Miller Reuben, jr. merchant S s Liberty b Strawberry al and 7th.
Miller David, clerk, N W c of 2d and Smithfield.
Moore Emmon, gent. N E c of Chancery lane and Front.
Moreland Adam, shoemaker, Miltenberger's Court.

Miller Thomas, carter, N E c of Marbury and Liberty.
Mountain Nancy, teacher, S s 2d b Ferry and Redoubt al.
Melatt Joseph, plough maker, do   do   do
Murphy Patrick, laborer, S s 2d b Ferry and Chancery lane.
Mehaffy Margaret, tailoress, S E c of 2d and   do
Montgomery Archibald, pilot, n 2d b market and Wood.
Marshall James, grocer, N s of the Diamond, E of Market.
Munion Terrence, labourer, N s Penn, b Garrison al and Wayne.
Morgan D. Morgan, blacksmith, Birmingham.
Miller John, labourer   do
Moss John, wagoner   do
Matters A.   do
Maffit John   do
Moore Clemson, blacksmith, Allegheny town.
Mason John, Esq.   do
Montgomery —— bagging weaver, Norther Liberties.
Mackeson John, engineer   do
Morrow Elizabeth, widow   do
Merton Arthur, wagoner   do
Moore Margaret, widow   do
Mann John, innkeeper   do
Metz Henry, butcher   do
Meichau Frederick, butcher   do
Megary Elizabeth, widow   do
Mercer Catharine, do   do
Montgomery John, weaver   do
Matthews William, roller   do
Montgomery Solomon, weaver   do
Moore Thomas, labourer, Kensington.
M'Donald John, labourer, E s Penn n Brewery al.
M'Weherter David, labourer, Point, old garrison.
M'Mullin John, labourer, Brewery al n Bell's al.
M'Bean Francis, grocer, N s Liberty, b Marbury and Bell's al.
M'Gahan Valentine B. teacher, W s Smithfield b 6th and Virgin al.
M'Dermott Thomas, merchant, E s Market b 5th and Liberty.
M'Farlane Jane, shop keeper, E s Market b Diamond and 5th.
M'Candless William, merchant and protho notary, office at the court
     house, store and dw W s Market, b 3d and 4th.
M'Kee David, grocer, S E c of Penn and Cecil's al.
M'Knight Wm. merchant, store W s Market n 4th, dw N s Liberty b
     Hay and Stevenson's al.
M'Combs John, tailor, N s 4th n Market.
M'Clurg & King, wholesale merchants, W s Wood b 3d and 4th.
M'Nickle John K. iron merchant, Water b Market and Chancery lane.
M'Cune Wm. sen. carpenter, N s of 5th b Wood and Smithfield.
M'Donald John, attorney, office S s Front n Market, dw in Water n
     Market st.
M'Elroy James, grocer, S E c of Wood and Diamond al.
M'Clelland Hugh, merchant, store E s of Market b 4th and the Dia-
     mond, dw S s 3d b Wood and Market.
M'Ilwaine Neal, coach maker, N s 5th b Wood and Market.
M'Gill & Darsie, cabinet makers, shop W s Wood b Front and 2d.

M'Gill John, cabinet maker, S s 3d b Wood and Smithfield.
M'Grew John, chair maker, S s 2d b Wood and Smithfield.
M'Intire William, carpenter, E s Union al b 6th and Strawberry al.
M'Fadden Thomas, read maker, W s St. Clair, b Liberty and Penn.
M'Clean James, grocer, S W c of Penn and St. Clair.
M'Clean George, shoemaker, W s St. Clair b Penn and Liberty.
M'Mahon Mary & Jane, mantua makers, No. 1, Gray's Row.
M'Dermott Mary, laundress, Barker's al n the Allegheny.
M'Cullion Michael, labour, Adams' al.
M'Henry Daniel, gent. S s Penn b Barker's al and Irwin st.
M'*Henry Wm.* blacksmith, shop S E c of Irwin and Penn.
M'Shane James, stone cutter, W s Irwin b Penn and the Allegheny.
M'Gunnigle Anthony, stone mason, E s Irwin b Penn do
M'Garagel John, labourer, do do do
M'Dowell John, teacher, N s Penn b Maddock's al and Irwin st.
M'Nulty Richard, labourer, Maddock's al.
M'Donald Wm. do do
M'Cormick James, labourer, N s Penn b Hand and Irwin's al.
M'Caddon Wm. tanner, N E c of do do
M'Grew Michael, shoemaker, S s Penn b *H*and and Garrison al.
M'Given James, labourer, S s Penn b Hand and Garrison al.
M'Guire Rev. Charles B. E c of Liberty and Cherry al.
M'Ayeal Robert, grocer, E s Wood b 6th and Liberty.
M'Elroy Charles, carpenter, N s Liberty b Garrison al and Wayne.
M'Cammon James, shoemaker, W s Wood b 4th and Diamond al.
M'Cormick John, merchant, E s Market b 5th and Liberty.
M'Masters *H*ugh, grocer, N s Diamond al b Wood and Smithfield.
M'Cully James & Co. grocers, N s Wood b 6th and Liberty.
M'Cracken James, salt inspector, N s Liberty, b Hand and Irwin's al.
M'Fadden Adams, clerk, at James Brown's
M'Conkey James, merchant, E s Market b 5th and Liberty.
M'Conkey Thomas, clerk, at M'Con*k*ey's Market st.
M'Candles Alexander, clerk, at U. S. Ban*k*.
M'Curdy James, drayman, N s 3d b Wood and Smithfield.
M'Phillemy Samuel, tobacconist, N E c of Liberty and Cecil's al.
M'Carty Susanna, milliner, W s Market b Front and Water.
M'Ilroy John, cotton manufacturer, E s Wood b Front and 2d.
M'Farlane Claudius, clerk, at John Sampson's, carpenter.
M'Ayeal John, at N. *H*olmes' porter cellar.
M'Masters & M'Intire, grocers, S W c of 6th and *W*ood.
M'Lean Archibald, pilot, N s Water, b Ferry and Chancery lane.
M'Kown Gilbert, clerk, n S W c of Cecil's al and Penn.
M'Kee David, Innkeeper, S E c of do do
M'Kee John, carpenter, do do do
M'Cool John, carter, S s Penn b St. Clair and Cecil's al.
M'Grew Alexander, carpenter, M'Masters' Court.
M'Quaid Peter, tailor, S s of Diamond al b Wood and Smithfield.
M'Cullough Joseph, carpenter, S s Virgin al b Wood and Smithfield.
M'Farlane John, doctor, S s 4th b *W*ood and Market.
M'Gregor Jane, S s 5th b   do
M'Cullough John, weaver, do   do
M'Candless Jane, widow, N s do do
M'Candless Anne, milliner, do do

M'Henry James, brick-layer, S s Penn b Irwin's al and Irwin's st.
M'Kee Thomas, carpenter, N s Liberty b Irwin's al and Hand st.
M'Callister John, pattern maker, N W c of Cherry al and 3d.
M'Millin Wm. tinner, S s Diamond al b Wood and the Diamond.
M'Affee Samuel, innkeeper, W s of St. Clair, b Penn and Liberty.
M'Kee & Graham, hatters, shop S E c of the Diamond.
M'Kee John, hatter, dw N s 4th b Wood and Market.
M'Guire John, plasterer, N E c of Redoubt al and 4th st.
M'Ilwaine Robert, grocer, S s Liberty b 7th and Strawberry al.
M'Cay James, innkeeper, E s of the Diamond, N of Diamond al.
M'Shane Hugh, com. merchant, S s Front b Market and Wood.
M'Ewen Washington, tailor, E s Marbury b Penn and Liberty.
M'Cague William, butcher, N s 6th b Smithfield and Church al.
M'Ginness John, tobacco manufacturer, S s of Liberty b Strawberry al
     and 7th st.
M'Curdy Jonathan, late constable, N s 3d b Market and Wood.
M'Curdy N. M. teacher, school N s of 4th opposite Ferry st.
M'Kenna Patrick, clerk, N E c of Ferry and Front.
M'Naughton Neal, boat builder, N s Water b Wood and Smithfield.
M'Farland & M'Lain, publishers of the Allegheny Democrat, W s
     Wood b 6th and Virgin al.
M'Farland Robert, watchmaker, N s Diamond al n Wood.
M'Kee John, innkeeper, N s Diamond al b Wood and Market.
M'Gowan William, sash maker, bank of the Allegheny b Garrison al
     and Hand st.
M'Gahan Jesse & Robert, coopers, N s 7th b Smithfield & Cherry al.
M'Cord Jane, teacher,   do   do   do
M'Clelland David, carpenter,   do   do   do
M'Donald James, labourer, N s Water b Grant and Ross.
M'Leod Catharine, widow, N s   do   n   do
M'Kinney Samuel, tailor, N s 2d b Grant and Ross.
M'Clelland Robert, labourer, N s 3d b   do
M'Elroy James, carpenter, S s 3d b   do
M'Callister Elizabeth, widow, N s Watson's road, E of High st.
M'Closky Barnard, blacksmith, N s Water, b Grant and Cherry al.
M'Cord John, wagoner, N W c of Grant and Water.
M'Crait —— widow, boarding house, N E c of 2d and Cherry al.
M'Ilhinny William, blacksmith, N s 2d b Wood and Smithfield.
M'Mullin William, grocer, N s Liberty, b Irwin's st. and Irwin's al.
M'Creary Susan, mantua-maker, E s Irwin b Penn and Liberty.
M'Lain Laughlin, shoemaker, do   do   do
M'Ilwaine & Boreland, wholesale grocers, N s Liberty b Hand and
     Irwin's al.
M'Cracken James, cotton spinner, N s Liberty b Hand and Irwin's al.
M'Cosh Samuel, gunsmith,   do   do   do
M'Nulty Biddy, widow, Church alley.
M'Mullin David, weaver, N W c of Church al and 6th.
M'Ferron William, labourer, N s 6th b Church al and Smithfield.
M'Cague Andrew, butcher, N s   do   do   do
M'Phillemy Isabella, seamstress, W s Smithfield b 6th & Strawberry al.
M'Farlane James, labourer, N s Strawberry al b Smithfield and Milten-
     berger's alley.
M'Clain David, jr. whitesmith, Cherry al b 6th and Strawberry al.

M'Birnie Margaret, seamstress, N s Strawberry al b Smithfield and Miltenberger's al.

M'Gahen Thomas, cooper, E s Miltenberger's al.

M'Clain David, sen. whitesmith, W s Cherry al b 6th & Strawberry al.

M'Affee Biddy, seamstress, W s Strawberry al b Cherry al & Miltenberger's al.

M'Ewen Miss Jane, seamstress, W s Cherry al b Strawberry al & 7th.

M'Keown Matthew, labourer, S s Strawberry al b Cherry al & Grant.

M'Intire Daniel, weaver, W s Smithfield b 6th and Virgin al.

M'Cullough Nancy, widow, S s 3d b Cherry al and Grant.

M'Camnis Francis, fireman, M'Clurg's Court.

M'Caslin James, weaver, S s Virgin al b Wood and Smithfield.

M'Nulty James, blacksmith, S s do do

M'Williams Robert, mason, N s 5th b Wood and Smithfield.

M'Dowell James, teacher, N s 2d b Wood and Market.

M'Collom William, laborer, S s Virgin al b Wood and Liberty.

M'Carty Teague, labourer, S W c of Virgin and Hillsborough al.

M'Mullin Alexander, weaver, S s of Diamond al b Liberty & Jail al.

M'Kee Stewart, painter, W s Jail al b Diamond al and 4th st.

M'Coy Alexander, blacksmith, S s 4th b Liberty and Ferry.

M'Cord Robert, wheelright, N s 4th b Jail al and Liberty.

M'Guire Margaret, tailoress, S s 4th b Market and Chancery lane.

M'Queen Thomas, teacher, S W c of the Diamond.

M'Gill William, tailor, S s Liberty b Virgin al and 6th.

M'Cargs Nathan, labourer, S s do do do

M'Donald Theophilus, gent. do do do

M'Kibben John, labourer, W s King's al.

M'Curdy David, carpenter, E s do

M'Carty James F. book-seller, N s Market b Front and Water.

M'Sherry John, tailor, shop E s Market b Front and 2d, dw N W c of Chancerry lane and Water.

M'Carty Isabella, widow, S s Front b Chancery lane and Market.

M'Carty James, packing box-maker, N s Front b Wood and Market.

M'Kee, Clarke & Co. com. merchants, S s Front b Wood and Market.

M'Cullough Adam, weaver, N s do do

M'Kinley Patrick, labourer, N E c Marbury and Liberty.

M'Donough Thomas, paver, S s of the Diamond W of market.

M'Kee David, blacksmith, N s 2d b Ferry and Redoubt al.

M'Quaid Patrick, laborer, S E c of Ferry and 2d.

M'Closky Michael, drayman, S W c of Chancery lane and 2d.

M'Cabe James, shop keeper, N s 2d b Wood and Market.

M'Callin James, laborer, E s Hillsborough al.

M'Clurg & Co. Pittsburgh foundry, S W c of 5th and Smithfield.

M'Kee John, glass blower, Birmingham.

M'Kee Mary, widow do

M'Intosh John, weaver, do

M'Intosh Joseph do do

M'Kelvy David, brick-maker, Allegheny town.

M'Cabe Alexander, labourer do

M'Ilhinny Robert, tanner do

M'Clean Samuel, tailor do

M'Vicker James, plasterer do

M'Ilwain John, rope maker do

M'Lenen Bernard, white lead maker, Northern Liberties.
M'Cullough Benjamin, shoemaker   do
M'Bane Catharine, grocer   do
M'Bride William, labourer   do
M'Nutt John   do   do
M'Clelland Joseph, carpenter   do
M'Ginn Bernard, butcher   do
M'Ilroy Samuel, nailor   do
M'Gown Samuel, brick maker   do
M'Kelvy Hugh,   do   do
M'Divitt Henry, tailor   do
M'Gin Matthew, butcher   do
M'Ginnis Bernard, labourer, Kensington.
M'Dowell James, glover   do
M'Donald Daniel, labourer   do
M'Kinny James, carpenter   do
M'Kee Thomas, nailor   do
M'Kinney James, blacksmith   do
M'Kee Jeremiah, engineer   do

N

NYMON PETER, wagoner, High street.
Nelson James, auger and sickle-maker, S E c of 7th and Miltenberger's alley.
Norman James, tailor, S s 3d b Wood and Market.
Nicholson Patrick, shoemaker, W s Wood b 4th and Diamond al.
Nimick William, grocer, E s Market b Front and Water.
Nealons Samuel, saddletree-maker, S s 5th b Wood and Smithfield.
Nesmith Thomas, lumber merchant, N s Penn b Irwin st and Barker's alley.
Nesbit Andrew, saddler, King's alley.
Neiper William, tailor, W s Grant b 2d and 3d.
Neal Hannah, gentlewoman, N s Front b Wood and Smithfield.
Neal Elliott, clerk,   do do   do   do
Nealons George, carpenter, S s Front b Grant and Ross.
Nealons Robert, saddletree-maker, do   do   do
Norris George, harness-maker, S s Front, b Cherry al and Grant.
Nutt James, Jr. wagon-maker, S W c of Liberty and 7th.
Nutt James, Sen. labourer,   do   do   do
Norris George, labourer, S s Strawberry, b Liberty and Smithfield.
Nicholas Edward, drayman, Bakewell's court.
Nixon John, engineer, High st.
Nicholson John, moulder, N s 3d b Grant and Ross.
Nutt Wm. engineer, E s Cherry al b Front and 2d.
Napier Margaret, shopkeeper, S s 3d b Grant st and Cherry alley.
Nixon Mary, widow, Water, b Wood and Smithfield.
Neff Abraham, carpenter, N s Liberty, b Irwin st and Irwin's al.
Norris Solomon, labourer, W s 5th b Wood and Smithfield.
Nichol Samuel, shoemaker, W s Market, b 5th and Liberty.
Nangle Mary, tailoress, c of Jail al and 4th st.
Nesbit Wm. gent. King,s alley.

12 *

Nerin Mary, laundress, E s Perry b Front and Water,
Newell Samuel, shoemaker, N s 2d b Wood and Market.
Neal Zenas, carter,   do   do   do
Newell Jane, seamstress,   do   do   do
Newhouse Jane, widow, N s 3d b Market and Wood.
Nichols Thomas, blacksmith, Birmingham.
Nesbit Wm, labourer, Allegheny town.
Nelson Wm. carpenter,   do
Newcombe Elisha,   N. Liberties.
Noland Elisha, farmer,   do
Neeland Evan, pudler,   do
Nicholson John, joiner, Kensington.

O

O'HARA MARY, gentlewoman, c of Water and West sts.
Otterman Lewis, fisherman, Brewery al n the Monongahela.
Orr James, blacksmith, S s 2d n Liberty.
Oliver Joseph, bellows-maker, S s 4th, below Smithfield.
O'Leary, Wm. glass-cutter, S s 2d b Smithfield and Cherry al
Ogden George, druggist, S E c of 2d and Wood.
Osborne John, constable, S s 4th b Wood and Smithfield.
Otterson Alexander, innkeeper, Union st.
Olver James, boarding-school, S s 4th, first door below Market.
Owens James, coach-maker, E s Grant, b 3d and 4th.
Oultsman Abraham, comb-maker, S s Diamond al b Wood & Smithf.
O'Handlin Susannah, shop-keeper, W s Wood, b 5th st and Diamond
      alley.
Owens James, shop-keeper, N E c of Penn and Irwin.
O'Brien Thomas, innkeeper, E s Irwin n Penn.
O'Brien John, carpenter,   do   do
O'Brien Joseph, plasterer,   do   do
Ormsby Oliver, gent. S E c of Grant and Front.
Outcalt Samuel, sparable maker, c of Church and Strawberry alley.
O'Donnell Charles, labourer, N s Strawberry, b Cherry and Miltenber-
      ger's alley.
O'Neal Henry, saddler, S s 2d b Wood and Smithfield.
O'Neal John, clerk, at Robert Knox's.
O'Donoughue Mary, widow, E s Smithfield, b Virgin alley and 6th.
O'Conner Thomas, feed-store, S s Liberty, b Virgin al and 6th.
O'Conner Catharine, widow, Water, b Ferry st and Redoubt alley.
O'Hara Catharine, widow, N s 3d, b   do   do
Obey John, grocer,   N. Liberties.
O'Callaghan Nicholas, chandler, do
O'Hern John, butcher, Allegheny town.
O'Neal James, rope-maker,   do
Orr John, carpenter,   do
O'Connor Dominick, clerk, Birmingham.

P

PARKINSON WILLIAM, innkeeper and ferryman, E c of Liberty and the Monongahela.

Perry John R. chairmaker or painter, at Parkinson's ferry.

Price Robert, ship carpenter, c of Brewery alley and Marbury st

Pedan Edward, N c of Liberty st and Cecil's al.

Payne Wm. labourer, S s Front, b Grant and Ross.

Park John, watchmaker, W s Wood below Diamond al.

Pride Mary, gentlewoman, N s Front b Cherry al and Grant.

Park J. & Co. grocers, S s 2d b Wood and Smithfield.

Park James, dw Smithfield c of Academy alley.

Patterson Joseph. esq. N s of Penn above St. Clair.

Peters Lewis, tanner, N s 4th E of Market.

Perkins Thomas, watchmaker, S s Market b Front and 2d.

Price Edward, saddler, N s 2d b Wood and Smithfield.

Patchell Gen. Edward, hatter, S W c of the Diamond.

Pentland Ephraim, esq.   do   do

Pratt Edward F. Barber, Jacksonian Head Quarters, W s Wood just below 5th, private establishment, S s Diamond alley b Wood and Smithfield.

Pentland Wm. esq. office in Court-house, dw N s 4th E of Market

Powers Thomas, cabinet maker, at Jos. Oliver's.

Pope Archibald, painter, S s Diamond al b Wood and Smithfield.

Patterson Roger, farrier, do   do   do   do

Park Alexander, innkeeper, N s of Diamond alley E of the Diamond.

Patterson John, carpenter, N E c of Water and Grant.

Peebles Robert, gent. at John Herron's.

Peppard Standish, grocer, Wood st b 4th and Diamond al.

Priestly N. W. grocer, S s Liberty, b Virgin al and 6th.

Patterson Rev. Robert, bookseller, S E c of the Diamond and Market st. dw in 4th b Wood and Market.

Pentland Alexander, tinner, S s 3d b Wood and Market.

Peterson Henry, tinner, S. W. c of Front and Market.

Peterson L. & P. tinners, N W c of do   do

Peterson Lewis, s. b. captain, N s 3d b Grant and Cherry alley.

Patterson Robert, merchant, N E side of the Diamond.

Parcell Abraham, carter, Maddock's alley.

Powers Benjamin, labourer, S s Strawberry al b Liberty and Smithf.

Pierce Sabra, widow   do   do   do

Patterson Martha, widow,   do   do

Pettigrew, Horner & Clayland, druggists, N E c of 3d and Market.

Pettigrew Samuel, dw N s 3d b Ferry street and Chancery lane.

Pinkerton Thomas, coachmaker, at Lecky's.

Peppard Patrick, grocer, E s Wood below Virgin alley.

Peter Robert, at Avery & Co's.

Paul Alexander, baker, N E c of Strawberry al and Liberty st.

Page John H. clerk, S E c of Grant and Front.

Porter James, labourer, E s Pitt n the Allegheny

Phillips James, wrought nailor, Bowen's alley.

Patterson Elizabeth, boarding house, S s Diamond al above Wood.

Price John, labourer,   do   do   do

Pentland Susan, gentlewoman, S s 4th E of Market.
Porterfield Jane, widow, W s Wood below 5th.
Patterson John, spooler, Stewart's court.
Phillipie Jacob, painter, S s Penn, b St. Clair st and Cecil's al.
Ploperd Andrew, drayman, Jackman's alley.
Phillips Stewart, blacksmith, E s Irwin b Penn and the Allegheny.
Phillips Samuel   do   Maddock's alley.
Powers Wm. labourer, N s Penn b Hand st and Garrison al.
Porter Joseph, brickmaker, do   do   do
Patton John, fisherman, S s Strawberry al b Liberty and Smithfield.
Peck Mary, boarding-house, Water, b Grant and Ross.
Paul Esther, widow, E s Grant b 2d and 3d.
Pride Matilda, gentlewoman, corner of Water and Smithfield.
Patterson John, water-hauler, N s Front, b Wood and Smithfield.
Park John, carpenter, N s 2d b   do   do   do
Parker William, weaver, E s Irwin b Penn and Liberty.
Patterson Robert N. pattern maker, N E c of Smithfield and Strawb.
Park James, labourer,   do   do   do
Pinkerton John, mason, Miltenberger's alley.
Patton Samuel, carpenter,   do   do
Pratt David, carpenter, E s Cherry al b 7th and Strawberry al.
Presly George, weaver, Harris' alley.
Palmer James, labourer, Toman's court.
Phillips Mary Ann, widow   do
Parsons Aaron, shoe-black N s 5th b Wood and Smithfield.
Perry Bernard, shoemaker, S s Liberty b Virgin al and 6th.
Palmer James, hatter, back from 5th, b Wood and Kings alley.
Plumer Wm & Co. saddlers, S E c of Market and 3d.
Palmer Henry, tailor, E s Market, b 2d and 3d.
Phillips John, shoemaker,   do   do
Petrie Alexander, tailor, N E c of Market snd 2d.
Pinkney Henry, boat builder, W s Ferry, b 2d and 3d.
Pollard John, hatter, Water b Ferry st and Redoubt alley.
Porter Samuel, blacksmith, S W corner of Chancery lane and Front.
Phelps Stephen, boarding house, N s Front W of Market.
Powers John, labourer, N s 3d c of Redoubt alley.
Patterson Robert, turner, S s 3d c of   do
Perchment Peter, ship-carpenter, S E c of Penn and Marbury sts.
Peters Ruth, baker, S s 2d b Ferry st and Chancery lane.
Park James, hatter, S E c of 2d st and Chancery lane.
Paxton James, blacksmith, N s 2d b Wood and Market
Patton David, labourer, Kensington.
Patchell Edward, brewer,   do
Pritchard Wm. forgeman,   do
Parson's John, cutler,   do
Packard Zibeon, nailor,   do
Piatt Benjamin, carpenter, Allegheny town.
Park James, labourer,   do
Porter Joseph, blacksmith,   do
Page Benjamin, glass-manufac. do
Patterson James, locksmith, Birmingham.
Patterson James, jr. do   do

Patterson George, cabinet maker, Birmingham.
Perry David, coal-digger.   do

Q

QUIGLEY EDWARD, boot and Shoemaker, W s Wood just above
    2d st.
Quigley Daniel, tailor, N s 2d b Grant and Cherry alley.

R

ROOK WILLIAM, blacksmith, Brewery alley near Marbury.
Read Martin, filer, W s Marbury n Penn.
Ream John, carter, S W c of Pitt and Penn.
Ream Solomon, carter, Killemoon's court.
Robinson Wm. shoemaker, N s Penn, b Cecil's alley and Pitt.
Richardson Wm. liquor store, W s of Wood, above Virgin alley.
Ross James, esq. attorney at law, 4th st above Grant.
Ross James, jr. esq. attorney,   do   do
Robinson John, carpenter, S s 2d b Wood and Market.
Richardson Nathaniel, merchant, S s 4th b do   do
Robinson William, gent. N W c of Wood and 4th.
Roseburg John, carpenter, S s Virgin alley, b Wood and Smithfield.
Roseburg Alex. do   do   do   do
Roseburg Samuel, do   Roseburgs court.
Richards Samuel, cabinet maker, W s Wood b 2d and 3d.
Rice William, blacksmith, S s Penn b Irwin st and Irwin's al.
Reiter George, confectioner, S s of Diamond al W of the Diamond.
Reed Thomas, labourer, S s Strawberry alley b Wood and Smithfield.
Robinson John, glass manufacturer, E s Ross n Second.
Robinson Thomas, grocer, E s Wood 2d door below 4th.
Robinson Richard, gent. N s Liberty b St. Clair and Cecil's alley.
Rowe Thomas, sen. blacksmith, N s 2d below Grant.
Rowe Thomas, jr.   do   do   do   do
Remington Stephen, carpenter, Penn above Hand st.
Rahm Martin, com. mer. N s 2d above Smithfield.
Rogers Mahlon, engineer, N W c of 3d and Grant, shop c of 4th and
    Grant.
Robinson James, grocer, W side Wood b 5th and Virgin al.
Ramsey John, proprietor of Mansion House Hotel, N corner of Wood
    and 5th streets.
Richmond Archibald, teacher, Richmond's court.
Roberts Edward J. attorney, N s 4th b Wood and Smithfield.
Read James, labourer, S s 2d b   do   do
Reed James, farrier and innkeeper, S s 5th W of Wood.
Riddle John S. com. mer. E s Wood, above Front.
Riley Terence, labourer, E s Pitt n the Allegheny.
Reddick Robert, coach-maker, E s Grant b 3d and 4th.
Richardson John, hosier, S s 5th b Wood and Smithfield.
Rineman Catharine, laundress, do   do   do
Ramsey William, labourer, S s do   do   do

Rowe Morris, shoemaker, E s Wood b Diamond alley and 4th.
Raymer Peter, grocer, W s Wood b 5th and Diamond al.
Rogers James, labourer, E s Irwin st b Penn and the Allegheny.
Rhinenart David, grocer, N s Penn b Irwin st and Irwin's al.
Rowan Charles, plasterer, Maddock's alley.
Richmond Ebenezer, filer, S s Hand below Penn.
Ritchie Allen, labourer, S s Strawberry al b Liberty and Smithfield.
Ritchie George, shoemaker, W s Liberty, b 7th and Strawberry al.
Ritchie Charles, labourer, do   do   do   do
Rutherford Agness, nurse, Irwin's al b Liberty and Penn.
Russell John, grocer, W s Liberty b Hand and Garrison al.
Ross Moses, cabinet maker, N E c of Liberty st and do
Rogers Martha, tailoress, S E c of Liberty and Smithfield.
Rulong James, carpenter, do   do   do
Rowley Mary, seamstress, S s Liberty above 7th.
Ritchie James, carpenter, N s 7th above Smithfield.
Read Daniel, wagoner,   do   do   do
Rogers Robert, lead manufacturer, Bakewell's court.
Roterick Abraham, carter, E s Grant b Front and Water.
Richards William, pudler, S s Front b Grant and Ross.
Robinson Joshua, glass-blower, N s do b do   do
Rutledge John, shoemaker, N s 2d b   do   do
Reed Wm. weaver,   do   do   do
Robinson Isabella, baker, S W c of Grant and 3d.
Robinson David, boarding house, S s Front b Grant and Cherry al.
Read John, carpenter, S s 3d b   do   do
Reno Charles S. freighter, E s Cherry al b 2 and 3d.
Reddick Samuel, labourer, Academy alley.
Rhodes Isaac, painter, Water, b Wood and Smithfield.
Rhodes Hanna, widow do   do   do
Riddle John, wagoner, W s 2d b Wood and Smithfield.
Ratcliffe Francis, labourer, N s 3d b do   do
Rippy John, tailor,   do   do   do
Royer John, iron merchant, do   do   do
Ralston Joseph, carpenter, E s Irwin b Penn and Liberty.
Reichter Henry, bricklayer, Church alley.
Richards George, bricklayer, 6th above Church alley.
Ritchie James labourer, S s 6th below Smithfield.
Robinson James, weaver, Smithfield b 6th and Strawberry al.
Robinson Robert do   do   do   do
Richard Andrew, labourer, N s Strawberry al n Miltenberger's al
Ramsey Robert, carter, Petticoat alley.
Ramsey John, carter, S s Strawberry n Cherry al.
Read John, tinner, E s Cherry alley b 6th and Strawberry.
Ray Martha, widow, do do   do   do   do
Read Thomas, labourer, N s Strawberry n Cherry al.
Rankin John, weaver, W s Smithfield, b Virgin alley and 6th.
Rogers John & George, tobacconists, S s 6th above Cherry al.
Ray John, weaver, Toman's court.
Roseberry Charles, bricklayer, Jail al. next the Jail.
Robinson Hugh, merchant, S E c of 5th and Market, dw in 5th next
    below Union
Rook Frederick C. shoemaker, S s Penn b St. Clair and Cecil's al

Robinson Julia, widow, King's alley.
Rippey John, tailor, E s market b Front and Water.
Robinson George, pilot, Chancery lane, b Front and Water.
Roberts Thomas, engineer, N W c of Chancery lane and Water st:
Richmond Henry, freighter, N s Front b Wood and market.
Reno Zachariah,   do   S s   do b market and Ferry.
Reynolds Lot, carpenter, S s 2d b Ferry st and Redoubt alley.
Reval Joseph, confectioner, N s 2d b market and Wood.
Reynolds Samuel, coal digger, Birmingham.
Robins Rachel, widow   do
Rankin William, millright, Northern Liberties.
Richardson Samuel, butcher   do
Robinson Richard, cotton weaver do
Reece Mary, widow   do
Richardson Samuel, chandler, Allegheny town.
Robinson William, jr. gent.   do
Rankin John, labourer   do
Richardson William, labourer   do
Ray William, mason   do
Richard George, butcher   do
Richards Ann, widow, Kensington.
Robin Richard, nailor   do
Reeder Josiah, roller   do
Rossetter John, nailor   do

S

SHAW WILLIAM, student, E s Bell's al.
Scaife Jeffery, tinner, E s Penn b Bell's al and Mononghela river
Shiras George, jr. brewer, at Point brewrey.
Shepherd John, grocer, S s Diamond al b Wood and Market.
Shiras George, sen. brewer, old garrison.
Sprague Alexander, carpenter, W s Marbury n Penn.
Scott Mary, laundress, c of Marbury and brewery al.
Sexton Richard M. blacksmith, S s 2d n Liberty.
Smith James, grocer, N s Diamond al b Wood and Market.
Sampson John, carpenter, N s Liberty b Garrison al and Wayne
Spear James, Innkeeper, S W c of Hand and Allegheny.
Shields James, paver, E s Smithfield, b 7th and Strawberry al.
Stewart James P. merchant, E s Wood b 3d and 4th.
Swartz George, merchant, E s Market b 5th and Liberty.
Swartz Horatio, clerk   do   do   do
Stoner Elizabeth, store keeper, E s Wood b 4th and Diamond al.
Stoner Solomon,   do   do   do do
Stevenson Hon. James S. N s Water b Wood and Smithfield.
Smith & Binny, engineers, E s High st.
Smith Matthew, engineer,   do
Stewart Matthew, register and recoder, S s 5th b Wood & Smithfield.
Simpson Robert, alderman, at Cotter's tavern, N E c of Front & Ferry.
Snowden John M. printer and mayor of the City, N s Liberty c of
    Irwin's al.
Snowden William, attorney, N s Liberty c of Irwin's al.

Scott William, plane ma*k*er, N s 4th n Wood.

Sheldon John S. book-binder, N s Diamond al b Wood & Smithfield.

Simmons Thomas, brick-layer, S s 2d b Grant and Ross.

Sewell James *H.* store keeper, S W c of Liberty and Market, dw S s 4th b Market and Ferry.

Shaler Charles, esq. Water b Short and West streets.

Sheriff John, tinner and coppersmith, E s of Market b 3d & 4th.

Sloan John, blac*k*smith, shop S s Penn b Bowen's al and St. Clair, dw W s Hillsborough al b 5th and Virgin al.

Stackhouse Mark, engineer, dw S E c of Water and Ferry.

Sturgeon Mary, grocer, N s Diamond al b Wood and market.

Stackhouse & Thompson, engineers, S s Liberty b 2d and Short st.

Stackhouse Samuel, engineer, S *W* c of Ferry and 3d.

Sutton George, Tuscaloosa manufacturer, N s Water b market & Wood

Sutton Alfred, merchant,   do   do   do

Snyder John, clerk, at the Pittsburgh bank, dw N W c of Penn and Hay st.

Scott James, innkeeper, W s Grant b 2d and 3d.

Scholy William, preacher, S s Diamond al b Wood and Smithfield.

Spear Daniel, merchant, N W c of Garrison al and Liberty.

Stewart Robert, proprietor of the Pittsburgh hotel and stage office, S E c of Wood and 3d.

Sands William, barber, N s 3d b Wood and market.

Stuart Jane, milliner, N s 6th b Wood and Church al.

Sawtell Joseph, merchant, N s Liberty, b Garrison al and Hand.

Siddle James, jr. cler*k*, N E c of Cherry al and Water.

Shannon Samuel, drayman, W s Smithfield b 6th and Strawberry al.

Swift Rev. Elisha, S s 4th b Cherry al and Grant.

Shaw Archibald, painter, N E c of Cherry al and Front.

Simpson W. A. doctor, S s 4th b Wood and market.

Sterr John, clerk, at Beal's in the Diamond.

Scott Samuel H. clerk, Ban*k* of Pittsburgh.

Stevenson George, whitesmith, E s Jail al b Liberty and Diamond al

Shidle James, paper stainer, at Anchor paper mill.

Stephenson Wm. baker, S E c of Liberty and Smithfield.

Stephenson *Wm.* jr. baker do   do

Scott George, brass founder, N s 2d b Wood and Smithfield.

Smith Alexander, inkeeper, N W c of Liberty and St. Clair.

Scully Dennis S. alderman, office S s of the Diamond W of market, dw N s 4th b Jail al and market.

Sutherland Hector, clerk, at Lindell's warehouse.

Spillane Thomas, grocer, S W c of Wood and 5th.

Snowden Henry, grocer, W s Wood b 5th and Diamond al.

Sproul & Russell, grocers, N s of Liberty, b Hand and Garrison a .

Smith N. R. teacher, N E c of Front and Chancery lane.

Stafford Henry, grocer, E s Diamond S of Diamond al.

Swartzwelder John, druggist, Bayard's Row, No. 5, dw N E c of Liberty and Garrison al.

St. John Samuel, hatter, E s Jail al opposite the Jail.

Stewart Charles, stage driver, at Pittsburgh Hotel.

Sellers Henry, doctor, N W c of 2d and Smithfield.

Sutherland John, labourer, at paper mill yard.

Stockton Jonathan, brick layer, Bowen's al.

Smith Margaret, seamstress, N s 4th b Wood and Smithfield.

Sweny Andrew, moulder, Richmond's court.

Scholy Mary, bonnet maker, S s Diamond al b Wood and Smithfield.

Smith Robert, labourer, S s Diamond al b Wood and Smithfield.

Spear James R. physician, office N s 4th b Wood and Market, dw S s 4th b   do   do

Sinnick John, shoemaker, N s 4th b Wood and Market.

Spencer Samuel, merchant, store E s Market b 4th and Diamond, dw N s 4th E of Market.

Scott Mary, seamstress, Stewart's court.

Scott James, carpenter,   do

Seawright —— labourer, S s 5th b Wood and Smithfield.

Smith John P. clerk, Water b Wood and Market.

Smith Susan, milliner,   do   do

Scott Walter, teacher, school No. 1, Gray's Row, residence Allegheny town.

Sutton James, labourer, Jackman's al.

Strawbridge James, cooper, W s Irwin b Penn and the Allegheny.

Shepherd James, labourer, E s Irwin, b Penn and Allegheny.

Shilletoe Thomas, labourer, Maddock's al.

Shepherd Asa B. carpenter,   do

Steele Robert, shoemaker, N s 3d b Grant and Cherry al.

Smith George, teacher, S s Penn b Hand and Garrison al.

Smith William, shoemaker,   do   do

Smith William, cooper,   do   do

Staly John, carpenter, W s Wayne n the river.

Sixe Andrew, hostler, N s Smithfield b 7th and Strawberry al.

Smith John, carter, N s Liberty, b Wayne and Garrison al.

Shepherd Patrick, labourer, Fayette al.

Sharp Robert, cooper, N s 7th b Smithfield and Cherry al.

Spear Alexander, carpenter, N s 7th b   do   do

Smith George, glass blower, Bakewell's court.

Smith Augustine, labourer, N s Water b Grant and Ross.

Smallman Joseph, labourer, do   do   do

Stewart Robert T. iron merchant, S s 2d b Ross and Grant.

Sidonspinner James, refiner, N s 2d   do   do

Stevenson James, clerk, E s Grant b 2d and 3d.

Stapleton Patrick, carter, S s 3d b Grant and Ross.

Shiner Elizabeth, laundress, do do   do

Sweny Thomas, moulder, E s High.

Smith Samuel, engineer,   do

Small Simon, carpenter, N s Watson's road n High.

Sowers Jacob, moulder do   do

Somers John, shoemaker, E s Ross b 3d and 4th.

Stevens Rev. William M. N s 3d b Grant and Ross.

Shaw James, plasterer, N s Front b Grant and Cherry al.

Smithson Miss Mary, milliner, S s Front b   do   do

Steelman Edward, glass blower, N s Front b Grant and Cherry al.

Smith William T. whitesmith, S s Water, next Bakewell's glass house.

Smith Margaret, midwife   do   do   do   do

Stewart Thomas, carpenter, E s Cherry al b Front and 2d.

Shinn Rev. Asa, E s Cherry al b 2d and 3d.

13

Sterrett William, carpenter, S *W* c of Cherry and Academy al.
Shultz John, carpenter, *W* s Cherry al   do   do
Steins Moses, carpenter, S s 3d b Wood and Smithfield.
Smith John, wool comber, N s of Liberty b Irwin st. and Irwin's al.
Street John, grocer, E s Irwin b Penn and Liberty.
Scott George, painter, E s Church al.
Seltzer Mary, laundress, *W* s Church alley.
Stewart Jane, seamstress,   do   do
Sands William, blacksmith, W s Church al.
Stewart John, painter, N s 6th b Church al and Wood
Sproat William, wagoner,   do   do   do   Smithfield.
Scott John, shoemaker,   do   do   do   do
Sawash Joseph, labourer,   do   do   do   do
Stewart William J. drayman, W s Smithfield, b 6th and Strawberry al.
Stevenson Rebecca, shoe binder, Petticoat al.
Shay Timothy, labourer, S E c of Smithfield and 6th.
Stewart James, cotton spinner, W s Foster's al b 6th & Strawberry al.
Saunders Anthony, coppersmith, W s Cherry al b Strawberry & 7th.
Stewart James, shoemaker, W s Smithfield b Virgin al and 6th.
Sharp Mary, tailoress, E s Carpenter's al.
Smith Robert, labourer, E s   do
Spear Alexander, weaver, W s Carpenter's al.
Syce Francis, labourer, W s Smithfield, b Virgin al and 6th.
Shaw Miss Eleanor, tailoress, W s Smithfield, b Virgin al and 6th.
Sheaffer Daniel, nailor, E s Smithfield   do   do
Seth Jacob, moulder, M'Clurg's court.
Stewart John, labourer,   do
Shaw Joseph, carpenter, S s Virgin al b Wood and Smithfield.
Stevens John, tailor,   do   do   do
Stevens Durham, fireman, N s 5th b Wood and Smithfield.
Sweeny Sarah, boarding house, Richmond's court.
Sackett Mary, seamstress, S E c of Virgin and King's al.
Stevenson Jane, shop keeper, S s Virgin al b Wood and Market.
Smith James, labourer, S s Virgin al b Wood and Smithfield.
Scully Humphry, labourer, Hillsborough al.
Smith Clarissa, laundress, W s Jail al next the Jail.
Sparr James M. pattern maker, N s 4th b Jail al and Liberty.
Sutcliffe Wm. machinist, S s 4th b Ferry and Chancery lane.
Smith James, saddler, S W c of the Diamond.
Strain Hugh, cooper, Jail al.
Semple Wm. M. merchant, E s Market b 5th and Liberty.
Swain Francis, shoemaker, S s Liberty b Virgin al and 6th.
Smith Thomas, tailor, N s 5th b King's and Hillsborough al.
Sinclair James, carpenter   do   do   do
Sampson Jane, seamstress   do   do   do
Staunton Wm. Lottery and Exchange office, W s Market b 2d & 3d.
Shannon Elizabeth, seamstress, S s 2d b Wood and Market.
Stewart John, blacksmith, W s Ferry b 3d and 4th.
Shanky James, labourer, E s Ferry b Front and 2d.
Swaney Patrick, grocer, S E c of Ferry and Front.
Stevens Mary, essence seller, N s Water b Ferry and Redoubt al.
Sample James, shoemaker, S W c of Chancery lane and Front.
Sample Jane, gentlewoman, N s Front b Wood and Market.

Sheridan William, blacksmith, E s Wood b Front and 2d.
Shields Alexander, teacher, school E s do do
St. Clair John, ship carpenter, N s Liberty, b Hay and Marbury.
Sigler Margaret, shop keeper, S E c of 2d and Chancery lane.
Sands John, clerk, N s 2d b Wood and Market.
Smith James, saddler, S W c of the Diamond.
Sterling Henry, merchant, N W c of Smithfield and Virgin al.
Shaw James, cotton manufacturer, Wood opposite Bayard's Row.
Sullivan Mason, carpenter, Birmingham.
Sugart Nathan, shoemaker do
Scott Nathan, blacksmith do
Shawhan Robert, farmer do
Schwartz Christopher do
Shewman David, shoemaker do
Shuper John, butcher do
Scott John, forgeman, Kensington.
Stewart Wilson, innkeeper, Allegheny town.
Saunderson John, butcher do
Stewart Lazarus, esq. do
Sawyer John, brickmaker do
Stockton Rev. Joseph do
Sample Thomas, tanner, do
Sturgeon Wm. plasterer do
Small William, stage driver do
Snider John, esq. do
Stoddard John, carpenter do
Stewart Robert, blacksmith do
Sloderback Jacob, bricklayer do
Stewart Thomas, carpenter do
Sweetland Nathan, machinist, Northern Liberties.
Scott James, carpenter do
Slaas David, weaver do
Shaffman John, founder do
Skiles Wm. labourer do
Stranahan David, brickmaker do
Sanderson James, butcher do
Sanderson Richard, do do
Scott Thomas, boot and shoemaker, do
Scott Josiah, carpenter do
Sweetland Ferdinand, machinist do
Seitz Christian, butcher do
Stevens James, pudler do
Stevens Edward, roller do
Scott John, labourer do

T

THOMPSON WILLIAM, weaver, S s Penn n Marbury.
Thompson Hugh, labourer, N s Liberty below Marbury.
Torrence Eleanor, widow, W s Smithfield, b Virgin al and 6th.
Trovillo Elijah, bricklayer, S s 6th n Wood.
Tobin William, labourer, W s Ross b Front and 2d.

Thaw John, clerk, at Bank U. S. dw E s Wood b 3d and 4th.
Taggart Jane, widow, N s 2d b Grant st and Cherry al.
Thompson Thomas, watchmaker, N s 4th b Market and Wood.
Todd George, carpenter, King's alley.
Thompson John, currier, N c of Liberty st and Barker's al.
Telfair John, blacksmith, S s Penn b St. Clair st and Cecil's al.
Taylor Rev. John, S E c of Liberty and 3d.
Tackaberry Thomas, comb-maker, S s Diamond al below Smithfield.
Taylor John, innkeeper, Irwin st n the Allegheny.
Taylor James, baker, N s 5th below Market.
Tannehill Walter, carpenter, N s 2d b Grant and Ross.
Thompson Adam, weaver, Virgin al above King's al.
Taylor Thomas, paper-maker, at Anchor mill yard.
Taylor Thomas P.   do   do   do
Taylor William   do   do   do
Tharp Aaron, Bowen's alley.
Tindall Minis, chair-maker, S s 5th E of Wood.
Tassey & Bissel, wholesale merchants, W s Wood b 2d & 3d.
Toner Meritt, carter, E s Irwin below Penn.
Telfair John, innkeeper, N s Penn, below Hand.
Thompson Moses, shoemaker, N s Penn n Hand.
Thompson John, labourer, S s Strawberry b Liberty and Smithfield.
Turner Rebecca, widow,   do   do   do   do
Taylor John, carpenter, N s Liberty b Wayne and Garrison alley.
Timmins Francis, cooper, S s Strawberry al b Smithfield and Liberty.
Trimble Robert, tailor, N s 7th, b Cherry al and Smithfield.
Thomas George, labourer, N s Front b Grant and Ross.
Taylor George, grocer, N E c of Wood and Water.
Thompson John, blacksmith, N W c of Smithfield and Water.
Tilly Agness, mantua maker, N s 3d b Wood and Smithfield.
Taylor James & Co. merchants, Liberty st opposite Bayard's Row.
Taylor Thomas, merchant, dw N s 3d b Wood and Smithfield.
Tolbert John, iron merchant, c of Liberty st and Irwin's al.
Taylor Francis, mason, Church alley.
Taylor John, bricklayer, Strawberry al E of Smithfield.
Troutwine Jacob, labourer, Miltenberger's alley.
Thompson James, engineer, S s Front E of Wood.
Toman Wm. carpenter, E s Smithfield b Virgin al and 5th.
Taggard John, shoemaker, Toman's court.
Tobin John, labourer, N s 5th below Smithfield.
Thompson Robert, filer, S s Diamond al n Liberty st.
Taylor Richard, ship-carpenter, N s 4th below Jail alley.
Twining H. M. teacher, S W c of the Diamond.
Thornhill Samuel, filer, Union st.
Tabor & Adderly, shoemakers, E s Market b 5th and the Diamond.
Tabor Rev. Joseph,   do
Torrence James, carpenter, S s Liberty b Market and 5th.
Trotter James, labourer, N E c of Virgin alley and Liberty st.
Torode John, tailor, E s Market, below 3d.
Townsend Robert, wire-worker, S E c of Market and 2d, dw in Front
below Ferry.
Townsend Reese C.   do   do   do   do
Tait Wm. saddler, W s Market b Front and 2d.

Thompson Isabella, widow, E s Ferry n Front.
Thomas Jacob, cooper, S s 2d b Ferry and Redoubt alley.
Thompson James, labourer, Hillsborough alley.
Taggart John & Co. grocers, N s Diamond al. E of Diamond.
Torney Mary, widow, N. Liberties.
Trimble Gibson, labourer, do
Taylor Thomas, pudler, do
Thomas George, labourer, do
Thompson Thomas, Kensington.
Tomina *Wilhelmina*, widow, Birmingham.
Troup George, baker, do
Thomas William, coal-digger do

U

UPPERMAN CONRAD, constable, inspector of flour, and innkeeper, S s Front above Wood.
Upperman Christopher, at Conrad Upperman's.
Updegraff Abner, whitesmith and auger-maker, S W c of 5th and Smithfield.
Upstall Edward, wagon maker, S s Smithfield, n 4th.
Utt Jemima, tailoress, Carpenter's alley.

V

VOGAN GEORGE, drayman, E s Marbury n Liberty.
Victor David, blacksmith, S s 2d n Liberty.
Varner James, baker and grocer, N c of 5th and Market.
Varner James, brewer, N s Liberty b St. Clair st and Barker's al.
Von Bonnhorst Charles, Alderman, office c of 5th and Union sts. dw c of 6th st and Cherry alley.
Volz Charles L. Merchant, E s Wood b Front and 2d.
Vail Penina, laundress, Bakewell's alley.
Vandegrift John, carpenter, *W*ater above Wood.
Vandiver Bernard, cotton spinner, Grant, b 7th and Strawberry alley
Vance John, drayman, Richmond's court.
Vandivender John, blacksmith, S s 5th above Wood.
Vance John, Hillsborough alley.
Varner Jeremiah, pilot, N s 4th below Jail alley.
Varner Samuel, pilot, W s Ferry b Front and 2d.
Vogan Thomas, labourer, S s 4th b Liberty and Ferry
Vandiver John, chairmaker, Birmingham.
Vetter Michael, shoemaker, Allegheny town.
Vance Andrew, labourer, do
Veneman John, labourer, N. Liberties.

W

WILEY ROBERT, shoemaker, W s Liberty n Ferry.
Woodruff Lewis, shoemaker, W s Liberty, n to the Ferry.
Wilson Robert, ship carpenter, E s Penn c of Brewery al.

13

Wightman William, ship carpenter, Brewery al n the Monongahela.
Watson Rachel S. grocer, S s Diamond al b Wood and Market.
Wilson Margaret, laundress, N s Liberty n Marbury.
Wynn Thomas, innkeeper, N E c of the Diamond and Market.
Watson William, stone cutter S s Front b wood and Smithfield.
Wilson James, hatter, shop E s Market b 3d and 4th, dw S s 3d b Wood and Market.
Wright William, stone cutter, W's Maddock's al.
Watson William, pump maker, N s Water b Wood and Smithfield.
Williams Robert, grocer, W s Smithfield b Front and 2d.
Willock William, Shoemaker, S s 2d b Wood and Market.
Willock Andrew, gent. W s Ferry b 2d and 3d.
Willock John,   do   do   do
Wickersham Isaac, wire worker, E s Market b Water and Front.
Wright Joseph, carter, E s Miltenberger's al b Strawberry al and 7th.
Warden and Arthurs, engineers, N E c of Short and 2d.
Warden John, engineer, N s 2d b Redoubt al and Short.
Woods Samuel, plasterer, W s Cherry al b Strawberry al and 7th.
Wright George G. cabinet maker, S's 4th b Wood and Smithfield.
Whitaker William, tailor, S s 2d b Ross and Grant.
Way Abishai, merchant, W's Market b 3d and 4th.
Wilkins Ross, deputy attorney general, S W c of Ferry and 4th.
Wilson Thomas, grocer, E s Wood b 6th and Liberty.
Williams Ralph, waiter, at J. S. Stevensons.
Woods William, gent. S s Liberty b Diamond al and 4th.
Whitton & M'Fann, grocers, W s Market b Diamond and 5th.
Whitton John, grocer, dw   do   do   do
Wilson John, freighter, S s 7th b Cherry al and Grant.
Wilson James, silversmith, at Heald's 2d st. dw N s Front b Grant and Ross st.
Ward Jesse, baker, S s Diamond al b Wood and Smithfield.
Wiley Daniel, clerk, at Mason and M'Donough's wholesale store.
Woods James R. printer, at John M'Farland's.
Walters Capernicus, saddler, E s Wood b 4th and the Diamond.
Wilson Samuel, freighter, at Mrs. Bracken's.
Welsh Joseph, innkeeper, S E c of Irwin and the Allegheny.
Wynne John, grocer and carter, N s Water, b Wood and Market st.
Williams John B. clerk, at Ramsey's Mansion House, dw W s St. Clair, b Penn and Liberty.
Wallace John, grocer, S s 5th b Wood and Smithfield.
Wrenshall John, merchant, S W c of Market and 4th st.
Webber Jeremiah, engineer, in paper mill yard.
Weaver John, paper maker,   do   do
Weeks Chauncey, nailor, Bowen's al.
Warden Samuel, labourer, N s Penn b Pitt and Cecil's al.
Wiley James, shoemaker, E s Cecil's al b Penn and Liberty.
Walter Ann, nurse, S's Diamand al b Wood and Smithfield.
Weaver Daniel L. tinner, N s Diamond al b Wood and Smithfield.
Wilson James, blacksmith, W s of Hand b Penn and Allegheny.
Walker Mrs. seamstress, Garrison al b Penn and Liberty.
Woods James, wire worker, S E c of Penn and Wayne.
Witty William, carpenter, S s Penn b Wayne and Washington.
Wright John, plasterer, S s Penn b Wayne and Garrison al.

Webb Edward, carpenter, W s Cherry al b Plumb al and 7th st.
West Susanna, laundress, S s Strawberry al b Liberty and Smithfield.
Wakefield Robert, shoemaker, W s Smithfield, b 7th & Strawberry al.
Wakefield Ann, milliner,   do   do   do
Watson Mary Ann, spinster   do   do   do
Wilson Eleanor,   do   do   do   do
Wolfe Jacob, shoemaker, N s Liberty b Hand and Garrison al.
Work Sarah, seamstress,   do   do   do   do
Wolfe Andrew, carpenter, N s Grant b Front and Water.
Ward William, nailor, S s Front b Grant and Ross.
Wilson Eliza S. milliner and mantua maker, E s Grant b 2d and 3d.
Wilson Joshua, bricklayer, S s 3d b Grant and Ross.
Witfield Nicholas, nailor, E s Hight st.
Watson   do   do   do
White Thomas, labourer, S s Front b Grant and Cherry al.
White Thomas, clerk, N s 3d   do   do   do
Wilkins Jane, nurse, S s 3d   do   do   do
Ware Cassilla, laundress, N s 3d b Wood and Smithfield.
Wybrandt John, merchant, S s Liberty b Market and Virgin al.
Weeks Joseph, grocer, No. 1, Bayard's Row.
Wightman James, grocer, E s Wood b Liberty and 6th.
Waters Oran, blacksmith, Irwin's al b Liberty and Penn.
White Mary, widow, W s Church al.
Wright James W. plasterer, W s Smithfield b 6th and Strawberry a!
Wigham John, shoemaker, W s   do   do   do
Wilson Eleanor, tailoress, Miltenberger's al.
Wilson Edward, labourer,   do
Waggoner John, tailor,   do
Wright Joseph, carter, W s   do
White John, potter, E s Strawberry al n Smithfield.
Walker James, carpenter, W s Foster's al.
Walker James, weaver,   do   do
Wyatt Robert, carpenter, N s Strawberry alley b Cherry alley and
    Miltenberger's al.
White John, carpenter, W s of Smithfield b Virgin al and 6th.
Watson Joseph, chair maker, W s   do   do   do
Woods John, blacksmith, W s Carpenter's al.
Weeks Silas, blacksmith, W s Smithfield b Front and Water.
Whannell Alexander, labourer, E s Smithfield b Virgin al and 6th.
Wright James, labourer, S s 6th b Smithfield and Cherry al.
Wilson Martha, widow, S s Virgin al b Wood and Smithfield.
White Samuel, labourer, S s Virgin al b Wood and Market.
Welsh John, labourer, W s Hillsborough al.
Williams Mary, gentlewoman, W s   do
Womelsdorf John, hatter, E s Jail al n 4th st.
Waugh J. Hoge, attorney, office E s Union b 5th and the Diamond.
Welsh Michael, cooper, W s Jail al.
Wilson John, commissioner, W s Union b 5th and the Diamond.
White Samuel, nailor, S s 5th b Union and Liberty.
Walker Robert, boat builder, W s Ferry b 2d and Front.
Winkler Edward, tobacconist, S s 2d b Ferry and Redoubt alley.
Wilson John, freighter, S s 7th b Cherry al and Grant.
Woods James, carpenter, S s Front b Ferry and Chancery lane.

Wickersham Elijah, wire worker, N s 3d near Ferry.
Wood Elizabeth, tailoress,   do   do
Wilson Thomas, shoemaker, N E c of Redoubt al and 3d.
Ward John, shoemaker, S E c of Ferry and 2d.
Warden Harriet, seamstress, S s 2d b Ferry and Chancery lane.
White A. shoemaker, W s Market b Front and 2d.
Wilson John, grocer, S s 3d b Wood and Market.
Warner Henry, clerk, S s   do   do
Wightman James, pudler,   Northern Liberties.
Wilson James, grocer   do
Whitten John H. butcher   do
Wolf William, butcher   do
Wright Thomas, engineer   do
Welsh Davidson, mason, Allegheny town.
Walker Isaac, brickmaker   do
Wilson Joseph, labourer   do
Woods Alexander, mason   do
Walkinshaw David, shoemaker   do
Wilson David, carpenter   do
Wendt Frederick, glass manufacturer, Birmingham.
Wilson George, labourer   do
Wendt Frederick, jr. glass manufacturer, do
Walker John, gent.   do
Watt James, forgeman, Kensington.
Watt James, labourer   do

Y

YOUNG JAMES, alderman, S s 6th below Smithfield.
Young John, cabinet maker, N E c of Liberty and Hand sts.
Young George, barber, W s Wood, below Diamond alley.
Young John W. constable, S s 6th below Smithfield.
Young Robert, sen. nailor, W s Wood below 6th.
Young Samuel, freighter, N s 5th, b Wood and Smithfield.
Young Edward, drayman, Garrison alley b Penn and Liberty.
Yost John, labourer, W side Wayne, n the Allegheny.
Young Sarah, widow, S s Liberty, b Virgin al and 6th.
Young John, boarding house, Ferry below 3d.
Young Elizabeth, widow, Hillsborough alley.
Young William, gent. S side 2d b Wood and Market.
Young James, freighter, do   do   do
Young Wm. shoemaker, N s of Diamond alley E of the Diamond.
Young Robert, wheelwright, S s 5th b Wood and Smithfield.
Yeo Sarah, widow,   Birmingham.
Yost Frederick, rope-maker, do
Yerkins-Anthony, ferryman, Allegheny town.
Young Conrad, butcher, N. Liberties.

Z

ZILLHART DAVID, gent. S s 3d b Grant and Ross.
Zimmerman Daniel, blacksmith, N. Liberties.

INDEX.

ADDITIONAL.

Fire Insurance Companies.

UNDER the head of *Fire*, we ommitted noticing the Fire Insurance Agencies in Pittsburgh. Of these there are FOUR, where Houses, Goods, Wares, Merchandize, &c. may be insured, viz.

American Fire Insurance Company—GEO. COCHRAN, of R'd. *Agent.*

Ætna   *do*   *do*   *do*   N. HOLMES, *Agent.*

Trader's Insurance   *do*   R. BOWEN, *Agent.*

Protection do   *do*   M. B. LOWRIE, *Agent.*

IN the list of practising Physicians, we omitted the names of Doctor SELLERS and Doctor BARBER.

Errata—In page 15, third line from the top, for " it would not be an extravagant," read " it would not be extravagant."

Johnston & Stockton,

BOOKSELLERS, PRINTERS & STATIONERS,

Market, between Second and Third streets,

PITTSBURGH,

KEEP CONSTANTLY ON HAND, A LARGE AND GENERAL ASSORT-
MENT OF

Miscellaneous, Classical, School & Blank

BOOKS.

Also, all kinds of Writing, Printing, Wrapping, and Tea

PAPER,

Which they will dispose of, wholesale and retail, on the
most reasonable terms.

THEY ALSO CONTINUE TO EXECUTE

BOOK & JOB PRINTING,

In a neat manner, and at the shortest notice.

Book Binding,

Executed in a handsome and substantial manner.

BLANK BOOKS, of every description, made
of good paper, and ruled to any pattern.

OLD BOOKS RE-BOUND.

J. & S. will give the highest price for clean Linen and Cotton RAGS, and Tanner's *Size Pieces*, delivered at their Paper Mill, Falls of Big Beaver, or at their Bookstore, Market street, Pittsburgh

June 1, 1826.

FASHIONABLE HAIR DRESSING,
BY
Pratt
Wood Street
Pittsburgh

OPPOSITE THE RUINS OF OUR LATE IMPERIAL RESIDENCE
and the ancient Temple of Innocence—a few doors
north of Solomon Lightcap's *Crack-loo* wagon
tavern, alias the *Lion's Den*.

Having again, notwithstanding the fluctuations of human affairs,
and the conflagrations of cities, established our head quarters on as
firm a basis as the nature of our domicil will admit—we have considered it proper, in order to consummate the great plan of increasing the comfort of our subjects, and at the same time to fulfil the
destinies of our art, to re-issue our manifesto and ancient decree, to
which we shall exact the strictest obedience, under no less a penalty
than the infliction of the three great curses of our art, viz:—a dull razor, cold water and stinking soap!

"*Be it enacted and decreed,* That no citizen, who may have the felicity to breathe the vital oxygen, within the influence of our beatific
administration, shall presume to act the part of "*Heautontimorumenos*"
or self-tormentor, by attempting our mystic operations with his own
sacrilegious hands; but that, henceforth, all who wish to be shaved,
either for the glorious and praiseworthy ambition of creating a beard,
or for the more comfortable purpose of getting rid of one, shall re-
pair at stated periods to the anti-chamber of our 'sanctum sanctorum,
or to one of the branches of the mother institution, which we have
established here and there, for the convenient, necessary and essen-
tial purpose of carrying on the operations of government; where the
sylphic hand of an adept is always ready to apply the mystic touch of
the razor, in such a manner, that the chin will be instantly as smooth
as the Belvidere, without the subject suspecting he had been under
the hands of an operator at all. And we do further order and decree, that during the raging of the dog-star, the functions of our *sa-
ble* deputies must cease, in order that the nasal faculties of our good
subjects may not be offended.—Let all obey!'

PRATT I.
AUTOCRAT & PRES'T OF THE A. O. OF SHAVING.

DAVIS & HANSON,

Auctioneers and Commission Merchants,

PITTSBURGH,

CORNER OF MARKET AND FRONT STREETS,

HAVE ALWAYS ON HAND A LARGE STOCK OF

FOREIGN & DOMESTIC

DRY GOODS,

GROCERIES, HARDWARE, AND QUEENSWARE:

AND

Pittsburgh Manufactured Articles,

Which they will sell at the lowest price for cash or acceptances.

ALSO

An Extensive Collection of

BOOKS,

In the various departments of Literature.

June 1, 1826.

Lock Manufactory.

J. & J. PATTERSON, Jr.

BIRMINGHAM, near Pittsburgh,

Take this method to inform the public, that their LOCK MANUFACTORY is in full and active operation,

WHERE ARE MANUFACTURED

Knob, Rim, Fine Plate and Banbury Stock Locks, from 6 to 12 inches.

ALSO

Best Norfolk Thumb Latches and Bolts,

Of a quality equal, if not superior, to any imported, which will be disposed of as low as can be brought from any of the eastern cities.

ALL orders for any of the above articles, addressed to the Manufactory—to *George Cochran,* Agent of the Pittsburgh Manufacturing Association, or to *Benjamin Darlington,* Market street, Pittsburgh, will be thankfully received, and promptly attended to.

Birmingham, June 1, 1826.

N. B. Large Locks for Banks or Prisons, made to any pattern.

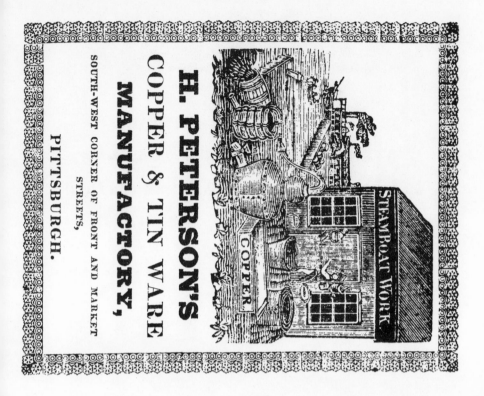

PETER BEARD,

Baker, Confectioner and Fruiterer,

Wood, between Third and Fourth streets,

PITTSBURGH,

Keeps constantly on hand, and FOR SALE, wholesale and retail,

Hard & Soft Bread, of all kinds, Confectionary, Fruits, Cordials, &c. &c.

He also keeps during the Summer season various Refreshments—as

ICE CREAM, LEMONADE, &c.

Parties and Assemblies furnished at the shortest notice, and on moderate terms.

June 1, 1826.

A. S. T. Mountain,

ATTORNEY AND COUNSELLOR AT LAW,

In Liberty, between St. Clair street and Cecil's
alley.

Reference—

JAMES ROSS, Esq.
WALTER FORWARD, Esq

June 1, 1826.

E. J. & S. A. Roberts,

Attorneys and Counsellors at Law,

AND

CONVEYANCERS,

Fourth street, three doors above Wood.

June 1, 1826.

M. S. Mason & M'Donough,

WOOD STREET,

PITTSBURGH,

HAVE ALWAYS ON HAND

An Extensive Assortment of

European, India and Domestic

DRY GOODS,

FOR SALE BY THE PACKAGE OR PIECE.

JOHN TORODE,

Merchant Tailor,

MARKET, BETWEEN SECOND AND THIRD STREETS

PITTSBURGH,

Keeps constantly on hand, a general assortment
of ready made Clothing, Shirts, &c.

June 1, 1826.

THOMAS HAZELTON

AGENT

PITTSBURGH.

MANUFACTURES

SCALE BEAMS,

P. BALANCES, LOCKS,

WHEEL IRONS, WINDOW FASTENINGS,

FACTORY SPINDLES,

AND A VARIETY OF WORK IN HIS LINE.

Orders executed faithfully and with despatch, if addressed to the MANUFACTORY, Liberty-street, or to GEORGE COCHRAN, Agent for the Pittsburgh Manufacturing Association, Wood-street; where merchants and others are invited to call, that they may examine for themselves.

June 1, 1826.